THE KEYES

Of the Kingdom of

HEAVEN,

AND

Power thereof, according to the
VVord of God.

BY

That Learned and Judicious Divine,
Mr. IOHN COTTON, Teacher of the Church
at *Boston* in *New-England*,

Tending to reconcile some present differences about

DISCIPLINE.

The second time Imprinted.

Gen. 13. 7, 8. *And Abraham said unto Lot, Let there be no strife, I pray, between thee, and mee; for we be Brethren.*
Gen. 45. 24. *And Joseph said to his Brethren (when they were going the third time out of Egypt) See that yee fall not out by the way.*
Acts 7. 26. *Sirs, yee be Brethren, why do ye wrong one to another?*
Eph. 4. 15. Ἀληθεύοντες ἐν Ἀγάπῃ, αὐξήσομεν εἰς αὐτόν, &c.

Published
By { THO. GOODWIN,
    PHILIP NYE.

London printed by *M. Simmons* for *Henry Overton*, and are to be sold at his shop in Popes-head-Alley. 1644.

Kessinger Publishing's
Rare Mystical Reprints

THOUSANDS OF SCARCE BOOKS
ON THESE AND OTHER SUBJECTS:

Freemasonry * Akashic * Alchemy * Alternative Health * Ancient Civilizations * Anthroposophy * Astrology * Astronomy * Aura * Bible Study * Cabalah * Cartomancy * Chakras * Clairvoyance * Comparative Religions * Divination * Druids * Eastern Thought * Egyptology * Esoterism * Essenes * Etheric * ESP * Gnosticism * Great White Brotherhood * Hermetics * Kabalah * Karma * Knights Templar * Kundalini * Magic * Meditation * Mediumship * Mesmerism * Metaphysics * Mithraism * Mystery Schools * Mysticism * Mythology * Numerology * Occultism * Palmistry * Pantheism * Parapsychology * Philosophy * Prosperity * Psychokinesis * Psychology * Pyramids * Qabalah * Reincarnation * Rosicrucian * Sacred Geometry * Secret Rituals * Secret Societies * Spiritism * Symbolism * Tarot * Telepathy * Theosophy * Transcendentalism * Upanishads * Vedanta * Wisdom * Yoga * *Plus Much More!*

<u>DOWNLOAD A FREE CATALOG</u>
AND
<u>SEARCH OUR TITLES AT:</u>

www.kessinger.net

Printing Statement:

Due to the very old age and scarcity of this book, many of the pages may be hard to read due to the blurring of the original text, possible missing pages, missing text and other issues beyond our control.

Because this is such an important and rare work, we believe it is best to reproduce this book regardless of its original condition.

Thank you for your understanding.

TO THE READER.

HE greatest commotions in Kingdomes have for the most part been raised and maintained for and about Power, and Liberties, of the Rulers and the Ruled, together with the due bounds and limits of either: And the like hath fallen out in Churches, and is continued to this day in the sharpest contentions (though now the seate of the warre is changed) who should be the first adequate, and compleat subject of that Church-power, which Christ hath left on earth; how bounded, and to whom committed. This controversie is in a speciall manner the lot of these present times: And now that most parties (that can pretend any thing towards it) have in severall ages had their turnes and vicissitudes of so long a possession of it, and their pleas for their severall pretences, have been so much and so long heard, it may well be hoped it is neere determining; and that Christ will shortly settle this power upon the right heires, to whom he primitively did bequeath it.

In those former darker times, this golden Ball was throwne up by the Clergy (so called) alone to run for among themselves: And as they quietly possessed the name Κλήρος, The Clergy, and of the Church, appropriated to themselves; so answerably all manner of interest in power or cognisance of matters of the Church, was wholly left and quitted to them: whilst the People that then knew not the Law, having given up their soules to an implicite faith in what was to be beleeved, did much more suffer themselves to be deprived of all Liberties in Church-affaires. This royall donation bestowed by Christ upon his Church, was taken up and placed in so high thrones of Bishops, Popes, Generall Councells, &c. Not onely far above these things on earth, the people; but things in Heaven also, we meane the Angels and Ministers of the Churches themselves; in so great a remotenesse from the people, that the least right or interest therein, was not so much as suspected to belong to them: But towards these latter times, after many removalls of it downe againe, and this at the issue of many suits againe and againe renued and removed, and upon the sentence (even of whole States) as oft reversed: It hath now in these our dayes been brought so neere unto the people, that they

To the Reader.

also have begun to plead and sue for a portion, and legacy bequeathed them in it. The Saints (in these knowing times) finding that the Key of knowledge hath so farre opened their hearts, that they see with their own eyes into the substantialls of Godlinesse, and that through the instruction and guidance of their teachers, they are enabled to understand for themselves such other things as they are to joyne in the practise of. They doe therefore further (many of them) begin more then to suspect, that some share in the Key of power should likewise appertain unto them.

It was the unhappinesse of those, who first in these latter times revived this plea of the peoples right, to erre on the other extreame (as it hath ever been the fate of truth, when it first ariseth in the Church, from under that long night of darknesse which Antichristianisme had brought upon the world, to have a long shadow of errour to accompany it) by laying the plea and claime on their behalfe unto the whole power; and that the Elders set over them did but exercise that power for them, which was properly theirs, and which Christ had (as they contended) radically and originally estated in the people onely.

But after that all titles have been pleaded, of those that are content with nothing but the whole, the finall judgement and sentence may (possibly) fall to be a sutable and due proportioned distribution and dispersion of this power into severall interests, and the whole to neither part. In Common-wealths, it is a Dispersion of severall portions of power and rights into severall hands, joyntly to concurre and agree in acts and processe of weight and moment, which causeth that healthfull update and constitution of them, which makes them lasting, and preserves their peace, when none of all sorts find they are excluded, but as they have a share of concernment, so that a fit measure of power or priviledge, is left and betrusted to them. And accordingly the wisedome of the first Constitutors of Common-wealths is most seene in such a just ballancing of power and priviledges, and besides also in setting the exact limits of that which is committed unto each; yea, and is more admired by us in this than in their other Lawes; and in experience, a cleare and distinct definement and confinement of all such parcells of power, both for the kind and extent of them, is judged to be as essentially necessary (if not more) than what ever other statutes, that set out the kinds and degrees of crimes or penalties.

So in that Politie or Government by which Christ would have his Churches ordered, the right disposall of the power therein (we humbly suppose) may lie in a due and proportioned allotment and dispersion (though not in the same measure and degree) into divers hands, according unto the severall concernments and interests that each rank in his Church may have; ra-

ther

To the Reader.

ther than in an intire and sole trust committed to any one man (though never so able) or any one sort or kinde of men or Officers, although diversified into never so many subordinations under one another. And in like manner, wee cannot but imagine, that Christ hath been as exact in setting forth the true bounds and limits of whatever portion of power he hath imparted unto any (if wee of this age could attaine rightly to discerne it) as he hath been in ordering what kinde of censures, and for what sinnes and what degrees of proceedings unto those censures; which wee finde he hath been punctuall in.

Now the scope which this grave and judicious Author in this his Treatise doth pursue, is, to lay forth the just lines and terriers of this division of Church-power, unto all the severall subjects of it ; to the end to allay the contentions now on foot, about it. And in generall he layes this fundamentall Maxime, that holds in common true of all the particulars, to whom any portion of power can be supposed to be committed : That look what ever power or right any of the possessors and subjects thereof may have, they have it each alike immediately (that is, in respect of a mediation of delegation or dependance on each other) from Christ, and so are each, the first subjects of that power that is allotted to them. And for the particular subjects themselves, he follows that division (in the handling of them) which the Controversie it selfe hath made unto his hands ; To wit, 1. What power each *single* Congregation (which is indowed with a Charter to be a body-politique to Christ) hath granted to it to exercise within it selfe : And 2. What measure, or rather, kinde of power Christ hath placed in Neighbour-Churches *without it*, and in association *with it*.

For the first. As hee supposeth each Congregation such, as to have the priviledge of injoying a Presbyterie, or companie of more or lesse Elders, proper unto it selfe ; so being thus Presbyterated, hee asserteth this incorporate body or societie to be the first and primary subject of a compleat and entire power within it selfe over its owne members ; yea, and the sole native subject of the power of Ordination and Excommunication, which is the highest Censure. And whereas this corporation consisteth both of Elders and Brethren, (for as for women and children, there is a speciall exception by a Statute-law of Christ against their injoyment of any part of this publique power ;) His scope is to demonstrate a distinct and severall share and interest of power, in matters of common concernment, vouchsafed to each of these, and dispersed among both, by Charter from the Lord : as in some of our Townes corporate, to a company of Aldermen, the Rulers, and a Common-Councell,

a body

To the Reader.

a body of the people, there useth to be the like: He giving unto the Elders or Presbytery a binding power of Rule and Authoritie proper and peculiar unto them; and unto the Brethren, distinct and apart, an interest of power and priviledge to concurre with them, and that such affaires should not be transacted, but with the joynt agreement of both, though out of a different right: so that as a Church of Brethren onely, could not proceed to any publique censures, without they have Elders over them, so nor in the Church have the Elders power to censure without the concurrence of the people; and likewise so, as each alone hath not power of Excommunicating the whole of either, though together they have power over any particular person or persons in each.

And because these particular Congregations, both Elders and People, may disagree and miscarry, and abuse this power committed to them; He therefore, secondly, asserteth an association or communion of Churches, sending their Elders and Messengers into a Synod, (so hee purposely chooseth to style those Assemblies of Elders which the Reformed Churches doe call Classes or Presbyteries, that so hee might distinguish them from those Presbyteries of Congregations before mentioned.) And acknowledgeth that it is an Ordinance of Christ, unto whom Christ hath (in relation to rectifying Mal-administrations and healing dissentions in particular Congregations, and the like cases) committed a due and just measure of power, suited and proportioned to those ends; and furnished them, not onely with abilitie to give counsell and advice, but further upon such occasions with a Ministeriall power and authoritie to determine, declare and injoyn such things as may tend to the reducing such Congregations to right order and peace. Onely in his bounding and defining this power, he affirmes it to be: First, for the kinde and qualitie of it, but a dogmaticall or doctrinall power, (though stamped with authoritie Ministeriall as an Ordinance of Christ) whether in judging of Controversies of faith (when they disturb the peace of particular Congregations, and which themselves finde too difficult for them) or in discerning matters of fact, and what censures they doe deserve: but not armed with authoritie and power of Excommunicating or delivering unto Satan, either the Congregations or the Members of them: But they in such cases, having declared and judged the nature of the offence, and admonished the peccant Churches, and discerned what they ought to doe with their offending members; they are to leave the formall act of this censure to that authoritie which can onely execute it, placed by Christ in those Churches themselves; which if they deny to doe, or persist in their miscarriage, then to

determine

determine to withdraw communion from them. And also for the extent of this power in such Assemblies and Association of Churches, he limits and confines that also unto cases, and with cautions (which will appeare in the Discourse) to wit, That they should not intrench or impaire the priviledge of intire Jurisdiction committed unto each Congregation, (as a libertie purchased them by Christs bloud) but to leave them free to the exercise and use thereof, untill they abuse that power, or are unable to manage it; and in that case onely to assist, guide, and direct them, and not take on them to administer it for them, but with them, and by them.

As for our selves, we are yet, neither afraid, nor ashamed to make profession (in the midst of all the high waves on both sides dashing on us) that the substance of this briefe Extract from the Authors larger Discourse, is, That very Middle-way (which in our Apologie we did in the generall intimate and intend) between that which is called Brownisme, and the Presbyteriall-government, as it is practised; whereof the one doth in effect put the chiefe (if not the whole) of the rule and government into the hands of the people, and drowns the Elders votes (who are but a few) in the major part of theirs: And the other, taking the chiefe and the principall parts of that rule (which we conceive is the due of each Congregation, the Elders and Brethren) into this Jurisdiction of a common Presbyterie of severall Congregations, doth thereby in like manner swallow up, not onely the interests of the people, but even the votes of the Elders of that Congregation concerned, in the major part thereof.

Neither let it seeme arrogance in us, but a testimony rather to the truth, further to Remonstrate, that this very Boundary platforme and disposement of Church-power, as here it is (we speake for the substance of it) set out and stated; as also that the tenure and exercise thereof in all these subjects, should be immediate from Christ unto them all, is not now new unto our thoughts; yea it is no other than what our owne apprehensions have been moulded into long since: And this many of our friends, and some that are of a differing opinion, having knowne our private judgements long, as likewise our owne Notes and transcripts written long agoe, can testifie; besides many publick professions since as occasion hath been offered: Insomuch as when we first read this of this learned Author (knowing what hath been the more generall current both of the practice and judgement of our Brethren for the Congregationall way) we confesse we were filled with wonderment at that Divine hand, that had thus led the judgements (without the least mutuall interchange or intimation of thoughts

or

To the Reader.

or notions in these particulars) of our Brethren there, and our selves (unworthy to be mentioned with them) here. Onely we crave leave of the reverend Author, and those Brethren that had the view of it, to declare: that we assent not to all expressions scattered up and downe, or all and every Assertion interwoven in it; yea, nor to all the grounds or allegations of Scriptures; nor should wee in all things perhaps have used the same terms to expresse the same materials by.

For instance, wee humbly conceive Prophecying (as the Scripture terms it) or speaking to the edification of the whole Church, may (sometimes) be performed by Brethren gifted, though not in Office as Elders of the Church; onely 1. Occasionally, not in an ordinary course. 2. By men of such abilities as are fit for Office: And 3. not assuming this of themselves, but judged such by those that have the power, and so allowed and designed to it: And 4. so as their Doctrine be subjected (for the judging of it) in an especiall manner to the Teaching Elders of that Church: And when it is thus cautioned, wee see no more incongruitie for such to speak to a point of Divinitie in a Congregation, then for men of like abilities to speak to, and debate of matters of Religion in an Assembly of Divines, which this reverend Author allows; and here, with us, is practised.

Againe, in all humilitie, wee yet see not that Assembly of Apostles, Elders, and Brethren, Acts 15. to have been a formall Synod, of Messengers, sent out of a set and combined association from neighbour Churches; but an Assembly of the Church of Jerusalem, and of the Messengers from the Church of Antioch alone; that were farre remote each from other, and electively now met: Nor are wee for the present convinced that the Apostles to the end to make this a Precedent of such a formall Synod, did act therein as Ordinary Elders, and not out of Apostolicall guidance and assistance; But wee rather conceive (if wee would simply consider the mutuall aspects which these two Churches and their Elders stood in this conjunction, abstracting from them that influence and impression which (that superior Sphere) the Apostles who were then present had in this transaction) this to have been a Consultation (as the learned Author doth also acknowledge it to have been in its first originall, onely rising up to be a Generall Councell by the Apostles presence, they being Elders of all the Churches;) or if you will, a reference by way of Arbitration for deciding of that great Controversie risen amongst them at Antioch, which they found to bee too difficult for themselves; and so to be a warrant indeede for all such wayes of communion between all, or any, especially neighbour Churches; and upon like occasions to bee Ordinances furnished with Ministeriall power for such ends and purposes. Our

To the Reader.

reasons for this, we are now many wayes bound up from giving the account of, in this way, and at this season; But however, if 't should have been so intended as the learned Author judgeth, and the Apostles *to have acted therein as ordinary Elders, yet the lines of that proportion of power that could be drawn from that pattern, would extend no further then a Ministeriall Doctrinall power, &c. in such Assemblies, which we willingly grant. And it may be observed with what a wary eye and exact aim he takes the latitude & elevation of that power there held forth, not daring to attribute the least, either for kind or degree, then what that example warrants, which was at utmost but a Doctrinall decernment, both of the truth of that controversie they were consulted in; as also the matter of fact in those that had taught the contrary, as belyers of them, and subverters of the faith; without so much as brandishing the sword and power of* Excommunication, *against those high and grosse delinquents, or others, that should not obey them in that Epistle.*

Only in the last place, for the further clearing the difference of the peoples intrest (which the reverend Author usually calleth Liberty, *sometimes* Power) *and the* Elders rule & authority (*which makes that first distribution of Church-power in particular Congregations) is likewise for the illustration of that other allotment of Ministeriall doctrinall power in an association or communion of Churches as severed from the power of* Excommunication (*which is the second.*) *We take the boldness to cast a weak beam of our dim light upon either of these; and to present how these have lain stated in our thoughts, to this end that we may haply prevent some readers mistake, especially about the former. For the first, we conceive the* Elders *and Brethren in each Congregation, as they are usually in the New Testament thus mentioned distinctly apart, and this when their meeting together is spoken of, so they make in each Congregation, two distinct intrests (though meeting in one Assembly) as the intrest of the* Common-Councell *or body of the people, in some Corporations, is distinct from that of the company of* Aldermen; *so as without the consent and concurrence of both nothing is esteemed as a Church act. But so as in this company of* Elders, *this power is properly* Authority; *but in the people there is a* priviledge *or power. An apparent difference between these two is evident to us by this: That two or three, or more select persons should be put into an Office, and betrusted with an intire intrest of power for a multitude, to which that multitude ought (by a command from Christ) to be subject and obedient as to an ordinance to guide them in their consent, and in whose sentence the ultimate formall Ministeriall act of binding or loosing should consist: this power must needs be esteemed and acknowledged in these few to have the proper notion and character of* Authority, *in comparison of that power (which must yet concurre with theirs) that is in a whole body or multitude of men, who have a greater and neerer interest and concernment in those affaires, over which these few are set as Rulers.*

This difference of power doth easily appear in comparing the severall interest of Father *and* Childe, *in his disposement of her in marriage, and her concurrence with him therein, (although we intend not the parallel between the things themselves.)*

To the Reader.

selves.) *A virgin daughter hath a power truly and properly so called, yea, and a power ultimately to dissent upon an unsatisfied dislike; yea, and it must be an act of her consent, that maketh the marriage valid: But yet, for her Parents to have a power to guide her in her choyce (which she ought in duty to obey) and a power which must also concur to bestow her, or the marriage is invalid, this (comparing her interest (wherein she is more neerly and intimately concerned) with theirs) doth arise to the notion of an* extrinsecall authority; *whereas that power which is in her, is but simply the power of her own act, in which her own concernment doth intrest her free by an* intrinsecall right. *The like difference would appeare if we had seen a Government tempered of an* Aristocracy *and* Democracy; *in which, suppose the people have a share, and their actuall consent is necessary to all lawes and sentences, whereas a few Nobles that are set over them (whose concernment is lesse generall) in whom the formall sanction of all should lye, in these it were* Rule *and* Authority, *in that multitude but* Power *and* intrest: *and such an Authority is to be given to a Presbytery of* Elders *in a particular Congregation, or else (as wee have long since been resolved,) all that is said in the New Testament about their* Rule, *and of the peoples* Obedience *to them, is to be looked upon but as Metaphors, and to hold no proportion with any substantiall reality of Rule and Government.*

And in this Distribution of power, Christ hath had a sutable and due regard unto the estate and condition of his Church; as now under the New Testament, he hath qualified & dignified it. Under the Old Testament, it was in its infancy, but it is comparatively come forth of its nonage, and grown up to a riper age (both as the tenure of the Covenant of grace in difference from the old, runs in the Prophets, and as Paul to the Galatians expresseth it.) They are therefore more generally able, if visible Saints (which is to be the subject matter of Churches under the N. Testament) to joyn with their Guides & Leaders in judging & discerning what concerns their own and their Brethrens consciences; and therefore Christ hath not now lodged the sole power of all Church matters solely and intirely in the Churches Tutors *&* Governors, *as of old when it was under age he did: But yet because of their weaknes & unskilfulnes (for the generality of them) in comparison to those whom he hath ascended to give gifts unto, on purpose for their guidance & the government of them; He hath therefore placed a* Rule *and* Authority *in those Officers over them, not directing only, but binding: so as not only nothing (in an ordinary way of Church-government) should be done without them, but not esteemed validly done unlesse done by them. And thus by means of this due and golden ballancing and poysing of power and interest,* Authority *and* Priviledge, *in* Elders *and the* Brethren, *this Government might neither degenerate into Lordlinesse and oppression in Rulers over the Flock, as not having all power in their hands alone; nor yet into Anarchy and confusion in the Flock among themselves; and so as all things belonging to mens consciences might be transacted to common edification, and satisfaction.*

For the second, Let it not seem a Paradoxe that a Ministeriall Doctrinall *Au-*

To the Reader.

thority should be found severed from that power of Excommunication, to second it, if not obeyed. Every Minister and Pastor hath in himself, alone, a Ministeriall Doctrinall authority over the whole Church that is his charge, and every person in it, to instruct, rebuke, exhort with all authority: *By reason of which, those under him are bound to obey him in the Lord, not only* vi materiæ, *by vertue of the matter of the commands, in that they are the commands of* Christ *(for so he should speak with no more authority then any other man; yea, a* Childe, *who speaking a truth out of the Word, should lead us, as the Prophet speaks;) But further, by reason of that Ministeriall authority which Christ hath indowed him withall, he is to be look'd at by them as an Ordinance of His, over them and towards them: And yet he alone hath not the authority of Excommunication in him, to inforce his Doctrine, if any do gainsay it: Neither therefore is this authority (as in him considered) to be judged vain and fruitlesse and effectuall, to draw men to obedience.*

Neither let it seem strange, that the power of this Censure, of cutting men off, and delivering them to Satan (in which the positive part (and indeed the controversie betwixt us and others,) of Excommunication lies) should be inseparably linked by Christ unto a particular Congregation, as the proper native priviledge hereof, so as that no Assembly or Company of Elders *justly presumed and granted to be more wise and judicious, should assume it to themselves, or sever the formall power thereof from the particular Congregations. For though it be hard to give the reason of Christs institutions; yet there is usually in the wayes of humane wisdome and reason, something analogous thereunto, which may serve to illustrate, if not to justifie this dispersion of intrests: And so (if we mistake not) there may be found even of this in the wisdome of our Ancestors, in the constitutions of this Kingdome; The sentencing to death of any subject in the kingdome, as it is the highest civill punishment, so of all other the neerest and exactest parallel to this in spiritualls, of cutting a soul off, and delivering it to Satan; yet the power of this high judgement is not put into the hands of an Assembly of Lawyers only, no, not of all the Judges themselves, men selected for wisdome, faithfulnesse, and gravity who yet are by office designed to have an intrest herein; But when they upon any speciall Cause of difficulty, for counsell and direction in such judgments do all meet, (as sometimes they do) yet they have not power to pronounce this sentence of death upon any man, without the concurrence of a Jury of his Peers, which are of his own rank: and in Corporations, of such as are Inhabitants of the same place: And with a Jury of these (men, of themselves not supposed to be so skilfull in the Laws, &c.) two Judges, yea, one, with other Justices on the Bench, hath power to adjudge and pronounce that which all of them, and all the Lawyers in this kingdome together, have not without a Jury. And we of this nation use to admire the care and wisdome of our Ancestors herein, and do esteem this priviledge of the Subject in this particular (peculiar to our Nation) as one of the glories of our Laws, and do make boast of it as such a liberty and security to each persons life, as (we think) no Nation*

about

To the Reader.

about us can shew the like. And what should be the reason of such a constitution but this (wich in the beginning we insisted on) the dispersion of power into severall hands, which in capitall matters, every mans triall should run through; whereof the one should have the tye of like common intrest to oblige them unto faithfulness; as the other should have skill and wisdome to guide them and direct therein.

And besides that intrest that is in any kind of Association, fraternity, yea, or neighbourhood, or like wise, that which is from the common case of men alike subjected to an Authority set over them to sentence them; there is also the speciall advantage of an exact knowledge of the fact in the haynous circumstances thereof; yea, and (in these cases) of the ordinary conversation of the person offending.

We need not inlarge the application of this: Although a greater Assembly of Elders are to be reverenced as more wise and able, then a few Elders with their single Congregations, and accordingly may have an higher doctrinall power, (a power properly, and peculiarly suited to their abilities) in cases of difficulty, to determine and direct Congregations in their way; yet Christ hath not betrusted them with that power He hath done the Congregations; because they are abstracted from the people: And so one Tribe of men concerned in all the forementioned respects is wanting, which Christ would have personally concurring, not by delegation or representation alone, not to the execution only, but even to the legall sentence also of cutting men off, as in the former parallel and instance may be observed. Yea, and the higher and the greater the association of the Presbyteries are, the farther are they removed from the people, and although you might have thereby a greater help, in that Juridicall knowledge of the Rule, to be proceeded by: yet they are in a farther distance (and disinabled thereby) from that precise practique knowledge of the Fact and frame of spirit in the person transgressing. And Cases may be as truly difficult and hard to be decided from obscurity, and want of light into the Circumstantiation of the Fact, and person, in which it was committed, and by him obstinately persisted in; as of the Law it self.

Other considerations of like weight might here be added, if not for the proofe (which we do not here intend) yet the cleering of this particular; As also to demonstrate that that other way of proceeding by withdrawing communion is most sutable to the relation, that by Christs endowment, all Churches stand in one towards another; yea, and wherein the least (being a body of Christ) doth stand unto all: But we should too much exceed the bounds of an Epistle, and too long detain the Reader from the fruitfull and pregnant labours of the worthy Author.

The God of Peace and Truth, sanctifie all the truths in it, to all those holy ends (and through his Grace much more) which the holy and peaceable spirit of the Author did intend.

THO. GOODWIN.
PHILIP NYE.

Of the Keys of the Kingdome of HEAVEN, and the Power thereof; according to the WORD of GOD, &c.

CHAP. I.

What the Keys of the Kingdome of Heaven be, and what their Power.

He Keys of the Kingdome of Heaven are promised by the Lord Jesus (the Head and King of his Church) unto *Peter*, Matth. 16. 19. *To thee* (saith Christ) *will I give the Keys of the Kingdome of Heaven: and whatsoever thou shalt bind on Earth, shall be bound in Heaven; and whatsoever thou shalt loose on Earth, shall be loosed in Heaven.* The words being Allegoricall, are therefore somewhat obscure: and holding forth honour and power in the Church, are therefore controversall; For where there is no honour (nor pride to pursue it) there is no contention. It will not therefore be amisse, for opening of the Doctrine of the Power of the Keys; somewhat to open the words of the Text, whereon that power is built. Five words require a little cleering.

Prov. 15. 1.

1. What is here meant by the Kingdome of Heaven?
2. What are the keys of this Kingdom, and the giving of them?
3. What are the acts of these Keys, which are said to be bindding and loosing?
4. What is the object of these acts to be bound or loos'd, here put under a generall name, *Whatsoever*?
5. Who is the subject recipient of this power, or to whom is this power given? *To thee will I give the Keys, &c.*

B   1. For

1. For the first: By the Kingdome of Heaven is here meant, both the Kingdome of Grace, which is the Church; and the Kingdome of Glory, which is in the highest heavens: For Christ giving to *Peter* the Keys of the Kingdome of Heaven, conveyeth therewith not only this Power to binde on earth (that is, in the Church on earth; for hee gave him no power at all to binde in the world; The Kingdome of Christ is not of this world:) but hee gives him also this priviledge; That what hee bound on earth, should be bound in heaven. And heaven being distinguished from the Church on earth, must needs be meant the Kingdome of Glory.

2. For the second: What the Keys of the kingdome of heaven be?

The Keys of the kingdome are the Ordinances which Christ hath instituted to be administred in his Church; as the preaching of the Word, (which is the opening and applying of it) also the administring of the Seals and Censures: For by the opening and applying of these, both the gates of the Church here, and of heaven hereafter, are opened or shut to the sons of men.

And the giving of these Keys, implyeth, that Christ investeth those to whom hee giveth them, with a power to open, and shut the gates of both. And this power lyeth, partly in their spirituall calling (whether it be their Office, or their Place and Order in the Church:) and partly in the concurse and co-operation of the Spirit of Christ, accompanying the right dispensation of these Keys; that is, of these Ordinances according to his will.

Moreover, these Keys are neither Sword nor Scepter; No Sword, for they convey not civill power of bodily life and death; nor Scepter, for they convey not Soveraigne or Legislative power over the Church; but stewardly and ministeriall. As the key of the House of *David* was given to *Hilkiah* (*Isa.* 22. 21.) who succeeded *Shebna* in his Office; and his Office was, עַל בַּיִת over the house *v.* 15. and the same word over the house, is translated Steward in the house, *Gen.* 43. 19.

3. Touching the third thing, What are the acts of these Keys?

The acts of these Keys are said here to be binding and loosing, which are not the proper acts of materiall Keys; for their acts be opening and shutting, which argueth the keys here spoken of be not materiall keys, but metaphoricall; and yet being keys, they have a power also of opening and shutting: for Christ, who hath the soveraigne power of these Keys, he is said to have the Key of *David*, to open, and no man to shut; to shut, and no man to open, *Rev.* 3. 7. which implyeth, that these Keys of Christs Kingdome have such a power of opening and shutting, as that they do thereby binde and loose, retain and remit; in opening, they loose, and remit; in shutting they binde, and retain; which will more appeare in opening the fourth point.

4. The fourth Point then is; What is the subject to be bound and loosed?

The Text in *Matth.* 16! 9. saith, *whatsoever*, which reacheth not (so far as the Papists would stretch it) to whatsoever oathes, or covenants, or contracts, or counsels, or lawes; as if whatsoever oaths of allegiance, covenants of lease or marriage, &c. the Pope ratifieth or dissolveth on earth, should be ratified or dissolved in heaven: No, this is not the Key of the Kingdome of Heaven, but the key of the bottomelesse pit, *Rev.* 9. 1. But this word, *whatsoever*, is here put in the Neuter Gender, (not in the Masculine, *whomsoever*) to imply both things and persons; Things, as sins; Persons, as those that commit them. For so, when our Saviour speaketh of the same acts of the same Keys (*Joh.* 20. 21.) hee explaineth himself thus: *Whose sins soever yee remit, they are remitted, and whose sins soever yee retain, they are retained.* Whatsoever you binde on earth, is as much therefore, as whose sins soever you retain on earth; and whatsoever you loose on earth, is as much as whose sins soever you loose on earth.

Now, this binding and loosing of whatsoever sins, in whosoever commit them, is partly in the conscience of the sinner, and partly in his outward estate in the Church, which is wont to be expressed in other terms, either *in foro interiori*, or *in foro exteriori*: As when in the dispensation of the Ordinances of God, a sinner is convinced to lie under the guilt of sin, then his sin is retained, his conscience is bound under the guilt of it, and himself bound under some Church-censure, according to the quality and desert of his offence; and if his sin be the more hainous, himself is shut out from the communion of the Church: But when a sinner repenteth of his sin, and confesseth it before the Lord, and (if it be known) before his people also, and then in the ministery of the Doctrine and Discipline of the Gospel, his sin is remitted, and his conscience loosed from the guilt of it, and himself hath open and free entrance, both unto the promise of the Gospel, and into the gates of the holy communion of the Church.

5. The fifth point to be explained, is, To whom is this power of the keyes given? The Text saith, to thee *Simon Peter*, the sonne of *Jona*, whom Christ blesseth, and pronounceth blessed upon his holy confession of Christ, the Sonne of the living God, and upon the same occasion promiseth both to use him and his confession, as an Instrument to lay the foundation of his Church; and also to give him the keys of his Church, for the well ordering and governing of it. But it hath proved a busie Question, How *Peter* is to be considered in receiving this power of the keys, whether as an Apostle, or as an Elder, (for an Elder also he was, 1 *Pet.* 5. 1.) or as a Beleever professing his faith before the Lord Jesus, and his fellow Brethren. Now because wee are as well studious of peace, as of truth, we will not leane to one of these interpretations, more than to another. Take any of them, it will not hinder our purpose in this ensuing Discourse, though (to speake ingenuously, and without offence what wee conceive) the sense of the words will be most full, if all the severall considerations be taken joyntly together. Take *Peter*, considered not onely as an Apostle, but an Elder also, yea, and a Believer too, professing his faith, all may well stand together. For there is a different power given to all these, to an Apostle, to an Elder, to a Believer, and *Peter* was all these, and received all the power which was given by Christ to any of these, or to all of these together. For as the Father sent Christ, so Christ sent *Peter* (as well as any Apostle) *cum amplitudine, & plenitudine potestatis*, (so far as either any Church-Officer, or the whole Church it self, was capable of it) *John* 20. 21. So that *Austin* did not mistake, when he said *Peter* received the keys in the name of the Church. Neverthelesse, wee from this place in *Mat.* 16. 19. will challenge no further power, either to the Presbyterie, or to the Fraternitie of the Church, then is more expresly granted to them in other Scriptures. Now in other Scriptures it appeareth; First, That Christ gave the Power of retaining or remitting of sins, (that is, the power of binding and loosing, the whole power of the keys) to all the Apostles as well as to *Peter*, *Iohn* 20. 21. 23. Secondly, It appeareth also, that the Apostles commended the rule and government of every particular church to the Elders (the Presbyterie) of that church, *Heb.* 13. 17. 1 *Tim.* 5. 17. And therefore Christ gave the power of the keys to them also. Thirdly, It appeareth farther, that Christ gave the power of the keys to the Body likewise of the Church, even to the Fraternitie with the Presbyterie.

For

For the Lord Jesus communicateth the power of binding and loosing to the Apostles, or Elders, together with the whole Church, when they are met in his Name, and agree together in the censure of an offender, *Matth.* 18. 17, 18. *If an offender (faith hee) neglect to heare the Church, let him be to thee as an Heathen or a Publican*, that is, let him be excommunicated. Which censure administred by them, with the whole Church, he ratifieth with this promise of the power of the Keys: *Verily I say unto you, Whatsoever you shall binde on earth, shall be bound in heaven, and whatsoever you shall loose on earth, shall be loosed in heaven.* In which place, howsoever there be some difference between Classicall and Congregationall Divines, what should be meant by the *Church* (*Tell the Church*) whether the Presbyterie or the Congregation; yet all agree in this, (and it is agreement in the truth, which we seek for) That no offender is to be excommunicated but with some concurse of the Congregation, at least by way: 1. Of consent to the sentence. 2. Of actuall execution of it, by withdrawing themselves from the offender so convicted and censured. Now this consent and concurse of the Congregation, which is requisite to the power and validitie of the censure, we conceive is some part of the exercise of the power of the Keys.

So that when Christ said to *Peter*, *To thee will I give the Keys of the kingdome of heaven*: If *Peter* then received the whole power of the Keys, then he stood in the roome and name of all such, as have received any part of the power of the Keys, whether Apostles or Elders, or Churches. Or, if hee stood in the roome of an Apostle only, yet that hindreth not, but that as hee there received the power of an Apostle, so the rest of the Apostles received the same power, either there, or elsewhere: and the Presbyterie of each Church received, if not there, yet elsewhere, the power belonging to their office: and in like sort each Church or Congregation of professed Believers, received that portion also of Church-power which belonged to them.

Chap. II.

Of the Distribution of the Keys, and their power, or of the severall sorts thereof.

The ordinary Distribution of the Keys, is wont to be thus delivered. There is *clavis* { 1. *Scientiæ,* A Key of knowledge, and a
{ 2. *Potestatis,* Key of power: and the Key

of power is $\begin{cases} 1.\ \textit{Ordinis,} \\ 2.\ \textit{Jurisdictionis,} \end{cases}$ Either a Key of Order, or a Key of Jurisdiction.

This distribution though it go for current both amongst Protestants and Papists; yet we crave leave to expresse, what in it doth not fully satisfie us. Foure things in it seeme defective to us:

1. That any Key of the Kingdom of heaven should be left without power: For here in this distribution, the Key of knowledge is contradistinguished from a Key of power.

2. There is a reall defect in omitting an integrall part of the keys, which is the key of Church-liberty. But no marvell, though the Popish Clergie omitted it, who have oppressed all Church-liberty: and Protestant Churches, having recovered the liberty of preaching the Gospel, and Ministery of the Sacraments, some of them have looked no farther, nor so much as discerned their defect of Church-libertie in point of Discipline: and others finding themselves wronged in withholding a key or power, which belongs to them, have wrested to themselves an undue power, which belongs not to them; the key of Authority.

3. There is another defect in the Distribution, in dividing the key of Order from the key of Jurisdiction; of purpose to make way for the power of Chancellours and Commissaries *in foro exteriori*: who, though they want the key of Order, (having never entred into holy orders, as they are called, or at most into the order of Deacons only, whereof our Lord spake nothing touching Jurisdiction) yet they have been invested with Jurisdiction, yea, and more then ministeriall authority, even above those Elders, who labour in word and doctrine: By this sacrilegious breach of order (which hath been, as it were, the breaking of the Files and Ranks in an Army,) Satan hath routed and ruined a great part of the liberty and purity of Churches, and of all the Ordinances of Christ in them.

4. A fourth defect (but yet the least, which wee observe in this Distribution) is, that order is appropriated to the Officers of the Church only. For though wee be far from allowing that sacrilegious usurpation of the Ministers Office, which wee heare of (to our griefe) to be practised in some places, that private Christians ordinarily take upon them to preach the Gospel publikely, and to minister Sacraments: yet we put a difference between Office and Order. Office wee looke at as peculiar to those, who are set apart for some peculiar Function in the Church, who are either Elders or Deacons. But Order (speaking of Church-order properly taken) is common

to all the members of the Church, whether Officers or private Brethren. There is an order as well in them that are subject, as in them that rule. There is a τάξις as well τῶν ὑποτακτικῶν, as τῶν ἐπιτακτικῶν. The maid in *Athens* is said, θεραπαίνης τάξιν ἐπιλάβεσαι, as well as her Mistresse. Yet if any man be willing to make office and order æquipollent, we will not contend about words, so there be no erroneous apprehension wrapt into the matter.

To come therefore to such a Distribution of the Keys as is more suitable to Scripture phrase. For it becomes true *Israelites* rather to speak the language of *Canaan*, then the language of *Ashdod*.

When *Paul* beheld, and rejoyced to behold, how the Church of *Colosse* had received the Lord Jesus, and walked in him; hee summeth up all their Church estate, *to wit*, their beautie and power, in these two, Faith and Order, Col. 2. 5, 6.

There is therefore a Key of Faith, and a Key of Order.

The Key of Faith, is the same which the Lord Jesus calleth the Key of knowledge, *Luke* 11. 52. and which hee complaineth, the Lawyers had taken away. Now that key of knowledge Christ speaketh of, was such, that if it had not been taken away, they that had it, had power by it to enter into the kingdome of heaven themselves, and it may be, to open the doore to others, to enter also. Now such a knowledge, whereby a man hath power to enter into heaven, is only Faith, which is often therefore called Knowledge, as *Isa.* 53. 11. *By the knowledge of him shall my righteous servant justifie many*: that is, by the faith of Christ. And *Joh* 17. 3. *This is eternall life to know thee*: that is, to believe on thee. This Key therefore, the Key of knowledge, (saving knowledge) or, which is all one, the Key of Faith, is common to all believers. A faithfull soule knowing the Scriptures, and Christ in them, receiveth Christ, and entreth through him into the kingdome of heaven, both here, and hereafter. Here he entreth into a state of grace through faith: and by the profession of his faith, he entreth also into the fellowship of the Church (which is the kingdome of heaven upon earth:) and by the same faith, as he believeth to Justification, so he maketh confession to salvation, which is perfected in the kingdome of glory, *Rom.* 10. 10.

The Key of Order is the power whereby every member of the Church walketh orderly himself, according to his place in the Church, and helpeth his brethren to walk orderly also.

It was that which the Apostles and Elders called upon *Paul*, so to carry himself before the *Jews* in the Temple, that he might make

it

it appear to all men that he walked orderly. (*Act.* 21. 18. 24.) Orderly, to wit, according to the orders of the Jewish Church, with whom he then conversed. And it was the commandement which *Paul* gave to the whole Church of Thessalonica, and to all the members of it, to *withdraw themselves from every brother that walketh disorderly*, 2 Thes. 3. 6. This their withdrawing from him that walked disorderly, was the exercise of their key of order. And it was a like exercise of the same key of order, when he requireth the Brethren to warne the *unruly*, which is, (in the originall) the same word, to admonish the *disorderly*: 1 Thes. 5. 14. And this key of order (to wit, order understood in this sense) is common to all the members of the Church, whether Elders or brethren.

Furthermore, of *Order* there be *two keyes*: a key of *power*, or *interest*: And the key of *Authority* or *Rule*. The first of these is termed in the Scriptures, *Liberty*: So distinguishing it from that part of *Rule* and *Authority* in the Officers of the Church. We speak not here of that spirituall libertie, whether of *impunitie*, whereby the children of God are set free by the bloud of Christ from Satan, hell, bondage of sin, curse of the Morall Law, and service of the Ceremoniall Law: nor of *immunitie*, whereby we have *power to be called the sons of God*, to come boldly unto the throne of grace in prayer, and as heirs of glory, to look for our inheritance in light: but of that *externall libertie*, or *interest* which Christ also hath purchased for his people, as libertie to enter into the fellowship of his Church, libertie to chuse and call well gifted men to office in that his Church: libertie to partake in Sacraments, or seals of the Covenant of the Church-libertie, and interest to joyn with officers in the due censure of offenders, and the like. This libertie and the acts thereof, are often exemplified in the Acts of the Apostles: and the Apostle *Paul* calleth it expresly by the name of libertie. *Brethren* (saith he) *you have been called unto LIBERTY, onely use not your libertie as an occasion to the flesh, but by love serve one another*, Galat. 5. 13. that the Apostle by that libertie meaneth Church-libertie, or power in ordering Church-affaires, will evidently appeare, if we consult with the context, rather then with Commenters. For the Apostle having spent the former part of the Epistle, partly in the confirmation of his calling, partly in disputation against justification by the works of the Law, to the end of *v.* 8. of Chap. 5. In the ninth Verse he descendeth not to exhort unto *bonos mores* in generall, (as usually Commenters take it) but to instruct in Church Discipline, in which

which he giveth three or foure directions to the tenth v. of *Chap.* 6.

1. Touching the censure of those corrupt Teachers, who had perverted and troubled them with that corrupt Doctrine of justification by works. *Chap.* 5. *ver.* 9. to the end of the Chapter.

2. Touching the gentle admonition and restoring of a brother fallen by infirmitie, *Chap.* 6. *ver.* 1. to 5.

3. Touching the maintenance of their Ministers, *ver.* 6, 7, 8. and beneficence to others, *ver.* 9, 10.

Touching the first, the censure of their corrupt Teachers. 1. He layeth for the ground of it (that which himself gave for the ground of the excommunication of the incestuous Corinth, 1 *Cor.* 5. 6.) *A little leaven leaveneth the whole lump*, *vers.* 9. 2. He presumeth the Church will be of the same mind with him, and concur in the censure of him that troubled them with corrupt doctrine, *v.* 10. (from fellowship with which corrupt doctrine he cleareth himself, *v.* 11.) 3. He proceedeth to declare, what censure he wisheth might be dispensed against him, and the rest of those corrupt Teachers. *I would* (saith he) *they were even cut off that trouble you*: cut off, to wit, by excommunication, *ver.* 12. Now lest it should be objected by the brethren of the Church: But what power have we to cut them off? The Apostle answereth, they have a power and libertie (to wit, to joyn with the sounder part of the *Presbyterie*, in casting them out, or cutting them off:) *For brethren* (saith he) *you are called unto libertie*.

If it should be further objected, Yea, but give the people this power and libertie in some cases, either to cast off their Teachers, or to cut them off, the people will soon take advantage to abuse this libertie unto much carnall licentiousnesse. The Apostle preventeth that with a word of wholsome counsell : *Brethren* (saith he) *you have been called unto libertie : onely use not your libertie as an occasion to the flesh, but by love serve one another*, *v.* 13. and thereupon seasonably pursueth this counsell with a caveat to beware of abusing this libertie to carnall contention, (an usuall disease of popular liberty) and withall dehorteth them from all other fruits of the flesh, to the end of the Chapter.

Evident therefore it is, that there is a key of power or liberty given to the Church (to the Brethren with the Elders) as to open a doore of entrance to the Ministers calling ; so to shut the doore of entrance against them in some cases, as when through corrupt and pernicious doctrine, they turn from Shepherds to become ravenous Wolves.

Having spoken then of that first key of order, namely, the key of *power,* (in a more large sense) or liberty in the *Church,* there remaineth the other *key of order,* which is the key of *Authority* or of *Rule,* in a more strict sense, which is in the *Elders* of the Church.

Authoritie is a morall power, in a superiour order, (or state) *binding or releasing an inferiour in point of subjection.*

This key when it was promised to *Peter,* Matth. 16. 19. and given to him with the rest of the Apostles, *Joh.* 20. 23. they thereby had power to bind and loose: and it is the same Authority which is given to their successours the Elders, whereby they are called to feed and rule the Church of God, as the Apostles had done before them, *Act.* 20. 28. And indeed by opening and applying the Law (the spirit of bondage accompanying the same) they bind sinners under the curse, and their consciences under guilt of sin, and fear of wrath, and shut the kingdom of heaven against them. And by opening and applying the Gospel (the Spirit of Adoption accompanying the same) they remit sin, and loose the consciences of beleeving repenting souls from guilt of sin, and open to them the doores of heaven. By vertue of this key, as they preach *with all authoritie,* not onely the doctrine of the Law, but also the Covenant of the Gospel; so they administer the seals thereof, Baptisme, and the Lords Supper. By vertue also of this key, they with the Church doe bind an obstinate offender under excommunication, *Matth.* 18. 17, 18. and releace, and forgive him upon his repentance, 2 *Cor.* 2. 7.

This Distribution of the *keyes,* and so of *spirituall power,* in the things of Christs kingdom, we have received from the Scripture. But if any men out of love to Antiquitie, doe rather affect to keep to the terms of the former more ancient Distribution (as there be who are as loath to change *Antiquos terminos verborum,* as *agrorum*) we would not stick upon the words rightly explained, out of desire both to judge and speake the same things with fellow-brethren. Onely then let them allow some spirituall power to the key of knowledge, though not Church-power. And in Church-power let them put in as well a *key of libertie,* that is, a power and priviledge *of interest,* as a *key of Authoritie.* And by their key of order, as they doe understand the key of office, so let them not divide from it the key of jurisdiction (for Christ hath given no jurisdiction, but to whom he hath given office) and so we willingly consent with them.

CHAP

Chap. III.

Of the subject of the power of the keys, to whom they are committed: and first of the key of Knowledge, and Order.

As the keys of the kingdom of heaven be divers, so are the subjects to whom they are committed, divers: as in the naturall body, diversitie of functions belongeth to diversitie of members.

1. The *key of knowledge* (or which is all one, the key of Faith) belongeth to all the faithfull, whether joyned to any particular Church or no. As in the primitive times, men of grown years were first called and converted to the faith, before they were received into the Church: And even now an Indian or Pagan may not be received into the Church, till he have first received the faith, and have made profession of it before the Lord, and the Church: which argueth, that the key of knowledge is given not onely to the Church, but to some before they enter into the Church. And yet to Christians for the Churches sake: that they who receive this grace of faith, by it may receive Christ and his benefits, and therewith may receive also this priviledge, to find an *open doore* set before them, to enter into the fellowship of the Church.

2. The *key of order* (speaking as we doe of Church order, as *Paul* doth, *Col.* 2. 5.) belongeth to all such, who are in Church order, whether *Elders* or *Brethren*. For though Elders be in a superiour order, by reason of their office, yet the brethren (over whom the Elders are made Overseers and Rulers) they stand also in an order, even in orderly subjection, according to the order of the Gospel. It is true, every faithfull soul that hath received a key of knowledge, is bound to watch over his neighbours soul, as his own, and to admonish him of his sin, unlesse he be a scorner: but this he doth, *Non ratione ordinis, sed intuitu charitatis*: not by vertue of a state of order which he is in (till in Church fellowship) but as of common Christian love and charitie. But every faithfull Christian who standeth in Church order is bound to doe the same, as well *respectu ordinis*, as *intuitu charitatis*, by vertue of that royall Law, not onely of love, but of Church order, *Matth.* 18. 15, 16, 17. whereby if his brother who offended him, doe not hearken to his conviction and admonition, he is then according to order, to proceed further, taking one or two with him: and if the offender refuse to heare them also then he is by order to tell the Church, and afterwards walk towards him, as God shall direct the Church to order it.

Chap. IV.

Of the subject to whom the Key of Church priviledge, power, or Libertie is given.

This key is given to the Brethren of the Church: for so saith the Apostle, in *Gal.* 5. 13. (in the place quoted and opened before) *Brethren, you have been called to liberty.*

And indeed, as it is the τὸ εἶναι, εὐεξία, & εὐπραξία, of a Commonwealth, the right and due establishment and ballancing of the *liberties* or *priviledges* of the people (which is in a true sense, may be called a *power*) and the *authority* of the Magistrates; so it is the safety of Church estate, the right and due setling and ordering of the holy *power* of the *priviledges* and *liberties* of the Brethren, and the ministeriall authority of the Elders. The Gospel alloweth no Church authority (or rule properly so called) to the Brethren, but reserveth that wholly to the Elders; and yet preventeth the tyranny and oligarchy, and exorbitancy of the Elders, by the large and firme establishment of the liberties of the Brethren, which ariseth to a *power* in them. *Bucers* axiome is here notable; *Potestas penes omnem Ecclesiam est, Authoritas ministerii penes Presbyteros & Episcopos.* In *Mat.* 16. 19. where *Potestas*, or *power* being contradistinguished from *Authoritas*, *Authori ie* is nothing else but a libertie or priviledge.

The liberties of the Brethren, or of the Church consisting of them, are many and great.

1. The Church of Brethren hath the *power*, *priviledges* and *liberty* to choose their Officers. In the choice of an Apostle into the place of *Judas*, the people went as far as humane vote and suffrage could goe. Out of 120. persons (*v.* 15.) they chose out, and presented two; out of which two (because an Apostle was to be designed immediately by God) God by lot chose one; And yet this one so chosen of God, συγκαταψηφισθῆ, *communibus omnium suffragiis inter duodecim Apostolos allectus est,* ver. 26. was counted amongst the Apostles by the common suffrages of them all. And this place *Cyprian* presseth amongst others, to confirm the *power* (that is ἐξουσίαν, or *priviledge*, or *liberty*) of the people in choosing or refusing their Ministers. *Plebs Christiana* (saith he) *vel maxime potestatem habet, vel dignos sacerdotes eligendi, vel indignos recusandi,* Epistol. 4. lib. 1.

The like, or greater liberty is generally approved by the best of our Divines (studious of Reformation) from *Act.* 14. 23.

They ordained them Elders, chosen by lifting up of hands.

The same *power* is clearly expressed in the choice of Deacons, *Act.* 6. 3. 5, 6. The Apostles did not choose the Deacons, but called the multitude together, and said unto them, *Brethren, look you out seven men amongst you, whom wee may appoint over this businesse: And the saying pleased the whole multitude, and they chose* Stephen, &c.

2 It is a *priviledge*, or a *liberty* the Church hath received, to send forth one or more of their Elders, as the publick service of Christ and of the Church may require. Thus *Epaphroditus* was a *Messenger* or *Apostle* of the Church of *Philippi* unto *Paul*, Phil. 2. 25.

3. The *Brethren* of the Church have *power* and *liberty* of propounding any just exception against such as offer themselves to be admitted unto their communion, or unto the seals of it: Hence *Saul*, when he offered himselfe to the communion of the Church at *Jerusalem*, was not at first admitted thereto, upon an exception taken against him by the *Disciples*, till that exception was removed, *Act.* 9. 26 27. and *Peter* did not admit the family of *Cornelius* to Baptisme, till he had inquired of the *Brethren*, if any of them had any exception against it, *Act.* 10. 47.

4. As the *Brethren* have a *power* of order, and the *priviledge* to expostulate with their *Brethren*, in case of private scandals, according to the rule, *Mat.* 18. 15, 16. So in case of publick scandall, the whole Church of *Brethren* have *power* and *priviledge* to joyn with the *Elders*, in inquiring, hearing, judging of publick scandals; so as to binde notorious offenders and impenitents under censure, and to forgive the repentant: For when Christ commandeth a brother, in case that offence cannot be healed privately, then *to tell the Church, Mat.* 18. 17. it necessarily implyeth that the Church must heare him, and inquire into the offence complained of, and judge of the offence as they find it upon inquiry. When the *Brethren* that were of the circumcision expostulated with *Peter* about his communion with *Cornelius*, and his uncircumcised family, *Peter* did not reject them, and their complaint against him, as transgressing the bounds of their just *power* and *priviledge*, but readily addressed himselfe to give satisfaction to them all, *Act.* 11. 2. to 18. The *Brethren of the Church of Corinth being gathered together with their Elders, in the name of the Lord Jesus, and with his power, did deliver the incestuous person to Satan,* 1 Cor. 5. 4, 5. And *Paul* reproveth them all, Brethren as well as Elders, that they had no sooner put him away from amongst them, *v.* 2. and expresly he alloweth to them all power *to judge* them that are within, *v.* 22.

Yea,

Yea, and from thence argueth, in all the Saints, even in the meanest of the Saints, an ability to judge between brethren, in the things of this life, as those that have received such a spirit of discerning from Christ, by which they shall one day judge the world, even Angels, so in the next Chapter, the 6. of that 1 *Cor.* 1.2,3,4,5. And the same *Brethren* of the same Church, as well as the *Elders*, he intreateth *to forgive* the same incestuous *Corinthian*, upon his repentance, 2 *Cor.* 2.7, 8.

If it be said, to *judge* is an act of rule; and to be Rulers of the Church, is not given to all the Brethren, but to the Elders onely: *Answ.* All judgement is not an act of authoritie or rule; for there is a judgement of discretion, by way of *priviledge*, as well as of authoritie by way of sentence: That of discretion is common to all the *Brethren*, as well as that of authority belongeth to the *Presbytery* of that Church. In *England*, the Jury by their verdict, as well as the Judge by his sentence, doe both of them judge the same malefactor; yet in the Jury their verdict is but an act of their popular liberty: In the Judge it is an act of his judiciall authoritie.

If it be demanded, What difference is there between these two?

The answer is ready, Great is the difference: for though the Jury have given up their judgement and verdict, yet the malefactor is not thereupon legally condemned, much lesse executed, but upon the sentence of the Judge: In like sort here, though the Brethren of the Church doe with one accord give up their vote and judgement for the censure of an offender, yet he is not thereby censured, till upon the sentence of the Presbytery.

If it be said again; Yea, but it is an act of authority to binde and loose, and the power to bind and loose, Christ gave to the whole Church, *Mat.* 18. 18.

Answ. The whole Church may be said to bind and loose, in that the Brethren consent, and concurre with the Elders, both before the Censure in discerning it to be just and equall, and in declaring their discernment, by lifting up of their hands, or by silence: and after the censure, in rejecting the offender censured from their wonted Communion. And yet their discerning or approving of the justice of the censure beforehand, is not a preventing of the Elders in their work. For the Elders before that have not onely privately examined the offender and his offence, and the proofes thereof, to prepare the matter and ripen it for the Churches cognizance: but doe also publickly revise the heads of all the materiall passages thereof before the

Church:

Church: and doe withall declare to the Church the counsell and will of God therein, that they may rightly discerne and approve what censure the Lord requireth to be administred in such a case. So that the peoples discerning and approving the justice of the censure before it be administred, ariseth from the Elders former instruction and direction of them therein: Whereunto the people give consent, in obedience to the will and rule of Christ. Hence is that speech of the Apostle; *We have in readinesse to revenge all disobedience, when your OBEDIENCE IS FULFILLED*, 2 Cor. 10. 6. The Apostles revenge of disobedience by way of reproofe in preaching, doth not follow the peoples obedience, but proceedeth whether the people obey it or no. It was therefore their revenge of disobedience by way of censure in discipline, which they had in readinesse, when the obedience of the Church is fulfilled in discerning and approving the Equitie of the Censure, which the Apostles or Elders have declared to them from the Word.

This power or priviledge of the Church in dealing in this sort with a scandalous offender, may not be limited only to a private brother offending, but may reach also to an offensive Elder. For (as hath been touched already) it is plaine that the Brethren of the Circumcision, supposing *Peter* to have given an offence in eating with men uncircumcised, they openly expostulated with him about his offence: and he stood not with them upon termes of his Apostleship, much lesse of his Eldership, but willingly submitted himselfe to give satisfaction to them all, *Act.* 11. 2. to 18. And *Paul* writeth to the Church of *Colosse*, to deal with *Archippus*, warning him to see to the fulfilling of his Ministery, *Col.* 4. 17. And very pregnant is his direction to the *Galatians*, for their proceeding to the utmost with their corrupt and scandalous false Teachers. *I would* (saith he) *they were even cut off that trouble you*; And that upon this very ground of their *libertie*, *Gal.* 5. 12, 13. as hath been opened above in *Chap.* 2.

But whether the Church hath power or libertie for proceeding to the utmost censure of their whole Presbytery, is a Question of more difficultie.

For 1. It cannot well be conceived that the whole Presbytery should be proceeded against, but that by reason of their strong influence into the hearts of many of the Brethren, a strong party of the Brethren will be ready to side with them: and in case of finding dissension and opposition, the Church ought not to proceed without consulting with the Synod. As when there arose dissension in the

Church at *Antioch*, and SIDING, (or as the word is ςάσις) they sent up to the Apostles and Elders at *Jerusalem*, who in way of Synod determined the businesse, *Act.* 15. 2. to 23. A precedent and pattern of due Church proceedings in case of dissension, when some take with one side, some with another. But of that more hereafter.

2. *Excommunication* is one of the *highest* acts of *Rule* in the Church, and therefore cannot be performed but by some Rulers. Now where all the Elders are culpable, there be no Rulers left in that Church to censure them. As therefore the Presbytery cannot excommunicate the whole Church, (though Apostate) for they must tell the Church, and joyn with the Church in that Censure: so neither can the Church excommunicate the whole *Presbytery*, because they have not received from Christ an office of rule, without their Officers.

If it be said, the *twenty-foure Elders* (who represent the private members of the Church, as the *foure living Creatures* doe the foure Officers) had all of them *Crowns* upon their heads, and *sate* upon *thrones* (*Rev.* 4. 4.) which are signes of regall authoritie: The answer is, The crowns and thrones argue them to be *Kings*, no more then their *white rayments* argue them to be *Priests*, ver. 4. but neither Priests nor Kings by Office, but by libertie to performe like spirituall duties by grace, which the other do by grace and office: As Priests they offer up spirituall sacrifices: and as Kings they rule their lusts, passions, themselves, and their families, yea, the world and Church also after a sort: the world, by improving it to spirituall advantage: and the Church, by appointing their own Officers, and likewise in censuring their offenders, not onely by their officers, (which is as much as Kings are wont to doe) but also by their own royall assent, which Kings are not wont to doe, but onely in the execution of Nobles.

But neverthelesse, though the Church want authoritie to excommunicate their Presbytery, yet they want not libertie to withdraw from them: For so *Paul* instructeth and beseecheth the Church of *Rome* (whom the holy Ghost foresaw would most stand in need of this counsell) to make use of this libertie: *I beseech you* (saith he) *mark such as cause divisions and offences, contrary to the* DOCTRINE *you have received*, ἐκκλίνατε ἀπ' αὐτῶν, WITHDRAW *from them.*

So then, by the agitation of this objection, there appeare two liberties of the Church more to be added to the former.

One is this (which is the fifth libertie in members) the Church hath

hath liberty in case of dissension amongst themselves to resort to a Synod. *Act.* 15. 1, 2. Where also it appeareth the *Brethren* enjoyed this libertie, to dispute their doubts till they were satisfied, *vers.* 7. 12. to joyn with the *Apostles* and *Elders* in the definitive sentence, and in the promulgation of the same. *vers.* 22, 23.

The sixth Libertie of the Church is, To withdraw from the communion of those, whom they want authority to excommunicate. For as they set up the Presbyterie, by professing their subjection to them in the Lord: so they avoid them by professed withdrawing their subjection from them according to God.

A seventh and last Liberty of the Church, is, Liberty of communion with other churches. Communion we say: for it is a great Libertie, that no particular church standeth in subjection to another particular church, no, not to a Cathedrall church; but that all the Churches injoy mutuall brotherly communion amongst themselves; which communion is mutually exercised amongst them seven ways, which for brevitie and memorie sake, we summe up in seven words. 1. By way of *Participation*. 2. Of *Recommendation*. 3. Of *Consultation*. 4. Of *Congregation* into a Synod. 5. Of *Contribution*. 6. Of *Admonition*. 7. Of *Propagation* or *Multiplication* of Churches.

1. By way of *Participation*; the members of one church occasionally coming to another church, where the Lords Supper cometh to be administred, are willingly admitted to partake with them at the Lords Supper, in case that neither themselves, nor the churches from whence they came, do lie under any publique offence. For wee receive the Lords Supper, not only as a Seal of our communion with the Lord Jesus, and with his members in our own Church, but also in all the churches of the Saints.

2. By way of *Recommendation*; Letters are sent from one church to another, recommending to their watchfulnesse and communion, any of their members, who by occasion of businesse, are for a time to reside amongst them. As *Paul* sent Letters of *Recommendation* to the Church of *Rome*, in the behalf of *Phœbe*, a Deaconesse of the Church of *Cenchrea*, Rom. 16. 1, 2. And of these kind of Letters hee speaketh to the Church of *Corinth* also though not as needfull to himself (who was well known to them) yet for others, 2 *Cor.* 3. 1.

But if a member of one church have just occasion to remove himself and his family, to take up his setled habitation in another church, then the Letters written by the church in his behalf, do recommend him to their perpetuall watchfulnesse and communion. And if the other church have no just cause to refuse him, they of his owne church do by those letters wholly dismisse him from themselves; wherupon the letters (for distinction sake) are called letters of dismission; which indeed doe not differ from the other, but in the durance of the recommendation, the one recommending him for a time, the other for ever.

3. By way of *Consultation*, one church hath liberty of communicating with another to require their judgement and counsell, touching any person or cause, wherewith they may be better acquainted then themselves. Thus the Church of *Antioch*, by their messengers, consulted with the Church at *Jerusalem*, touching the necessitie of circumcision, *Acts* 15. 3. although the consultation brought forth a further effect of communion with churches; to wit, their Congregation into a Synod. Which is the fourth way of communion of churches: All of the churches have the like libertie of sending their messengers to debate and determine in a Synod, such matters as do concern them all; As the Church of *Antioch* sent messengers to *Ierusalem* for resolution and satisfaction in a doubt that troubled them: the like libertie by proportion might any other church have taken, yea, many churches together; yea, all the churches in the world, in any case that might concern them all. What authoritie these Synods have received, and may put forth, will come to be considered in the sequele.

A fifth way of communion of churches, is the Libertie of giving and receiving mutuall supplies and succours one from another. The Church at *Ierusalem* communicated to the churches of the *Gentiles*, their spirituall treasures of gifts of Grace; and the churches of the *Gentiles* ministred back again to them, liberall oblations of outward beneficence, *Rom.* 15. 26, 27. *Acts* 11. 29, 30. When the church of *Antioch* aboundeth with more varietie of spirituall gifted men, then the state of their own church stood in neeed of; they fasted and prayed; as for other ends, so for the inlargement of Chrifts Kingdome in the improvement of them. And the Holy Ghoft opened them a dore for the succour of many countreys about them, by the sending forth of some of them, *Acts* 13. 1, 2, 3.

A sixth way of communion of churches is by way of mutuall admonition, when a publike offence is found amongst any of them: For as *Paul* had liberty to admonish *Peter* before the whole church at *Antioch*, when hee saw him walk not with a right foot, (and yet

Paul

Paul had no authority over *Peter*, but onely both of them had equall mutuall interest one in another) *Gal.* 2. 11. to 14. So by the same proportion, one Church hath liberty to admonish another, though they be both of them of equall authority; seeing one Church hath as much interest in another, as one Apostle in another. And if by the royall law of love, one Brother hath liberty to admonish his Brother in the same Church, (*Mat.* 18. 15, 16.) then by the same rule of brotherly love, and mutual watchfulnes, one Church hath power to admonish another, in faithfulnesse to the Lord, and unto them. The Church in the *Canticles* took care not only for her own members, but for her little sister, which she thought had no breast; yea, and consulteth with other Churches what to doe for her, *Cant.* 8. 8. And would she not then have taken like care, in case their little sister having breasts, her breasts had been distempered, and given corrupt matter in stead of milk?

A seventh way of communion of Churches may bee by way of propagation and multiplication of Churches: As when a particular Church of Christ shall grow so full of members, as all of them cannot heare the voice of their Ministers; then as an Hive full of Bees swarmeth forth, so is the Church occasioned to send forth a sufficient number of her members, fit to enter into a Church-state, and to carry along Church-work amongst themselves. And for that end they either send forth some one or other of their Elders with them, or direct them where to procure such to come unto them. The like course is wont to be taken, when sundry Christians comming over from one countrey to another; such as are come over first, and are themselves full of company, direct those that come after them, and assist them in like sort, in the combination of themselves into Church-order, according to the Rule of the Gospel. Though the Apostles be dead, whose office it was to plant, and gather, and multiply Churches; yet the work is not dead, but the same power of the keyes is left with the Churches in common, and with each particular Church for her part, according to their measure, to propagate and enlarge the Kingdome of Christ (as God shall give opportunity) throughout all generations.

CHAP.

Chap. V.
Of the subject to whom the Key of Authority is committed.

The key of *Authority* or *Rule*, is committed to the Elders of the Church, and so the act of Rule is made the proper act of their office, *The Elders that rule well*, &c. 1 Tim. 5. 17. Heb. 13. 7, 17.

The speciall acts of this rule are many.

The first and principall is that which the *Elders who labour in the Word and Doctrine*, are chiefly to attend unto, that is, the *preaching of the Word with all Authority*, and that which is annexed thereto, the administration of the Sacraments, or Seales, *Speak, rebuke and exhort* (saith *Paul* to *Titus*) *with all authority*, Tit. 2. 15. And that the administration of the seals is annexed thereto, is plain from *Matth.* 28. 19, 20. *Go* (saith Christ to the Apostles) *make Disciples, and baptize them*, &c.

If it be objected, Private members may all of them prophecie publickly, 1 *Cor.* 14. 31. and therefore also baptize: and so this act of authority is not peculiar to preaching Elders.

Ans. 1. The place in the Corinths doth not speak of ordinarie private members, but of men furnished with extraordinary gifts. Kings at the time of their Coronation give many extraordinarie large gifts, which they do not daily poure out in like sort in their ordinary government. Christ soon after his ascension poured out a larger measure of his Spirit then in times succeeding. The members of the Church of Corinth (as of many other in those primitive times) were *inriched with all knowledge, and in all utterance*, 1 *Cor.* 1. 5. And the same persons that had the *gift of prophesie* in the Church of Corinth, had also *the gift of Tongues*, which put upon the Apostle a necessity to take them off from their frequent speaking with Tongues, by preferring prophesie before it, 1 *Cor.* 14. 2. to 24. So that though all they might prophesie (as having extraordinary gifts for it,) yet the like liberty is not allowed to them that want the like gifts. In the *Church of Israel*, none besides the *Priests* and *Levites*, did ordinarily prophesie, either in the Temple, or in the Synagogues, unlesse they were either furnished with extraordinary gifts of prophesie, (as the Prophets of *Israel*) or were set apart, and trained up, to prepare for such a calling, *as the sonnes of the Prophets*. When *Amos* was forbidden by the *high Priest* of *Bethel*, to prophesie at *Bethel*, *Amos* doth not alledge nor plead

and the Power thereof.

the liberty of any *Israelite* to prophesie in the holy Assemblies, but alledgeth onely his extraordinary calling, *Amos* 7. 14, 15. It appeareth also that the *sons of the Prophets*, that is, men set apart and trained up to prepare for that calling, were allowed the like libertie, 1 *Sam.* 19. 20.

Answ. 2. But neither the sons of the Prophets, nor the Prophets themselves, were wont to offer sacrifices in Israel, (except *Samuel* and *Eliah* by special direction) nor did the extraordinarie Prophets in Corinth take upon them to administer Sacraments.

If any reply, That if the Prophets in the Church at Corinth had been endued with extraordinary gifts of prophesie they had not been *subject* to the *judgment of the Prophets*, which these are directed to be, 1. *Cor.* 14. 22.

Answ. It followeth not. For the People of God were to examine all prophesies, *by the Law and Testimony*, and not to receive them but according to that rule, *Psal.* 8. 20. Yea and *Paul* himself referreth all his Doctrine *to the Law and Prophets*, *Acts* 26. 21. And the Bereans are commended for examining *Pauls* Doctrine according to the Scriptures, *Acts* 17. 11, 12.

2. A second act of Authoritie common to the Elders, is, they have power, as any weighty occasion shall require, *to call the Church together, as the Apostles called the Church together* for the election of Deacons, *Acts* 6. 2. And in like sort are the *Priests* of the old Testament stirred up to call a solemne Assembly, to gather the Elders, and all the inhabitants of the land, to *sanctifie a Fast, Joel* 1. 13, 14.

3. It is an act of their power, to examine, if the Apostles, then any others (whether officers or members) before they be received of the Church, *Rev* 2. 2.

A fourth act of their rule is, the *Ordination of Officers* (whom the people have chosen) whether Elders or Deacons, 1 *Tim.* 4. 14. *Acts* 6. 6.

5. It is an act of the *Key of Authority*, that the Elders *open the doores of Speech and Silence* in the Assembly. They were the *Rulers of the Synagogue*, who sent to *Paul* and *Barnabas* to open their mouthes in a *word of exhortation*, Acts 13. 15. and it is the same power which calleth men to speak, to put men to silence when they speak amisse. And yet when the *Elders* themselves do lie under offence, or under suspition of it, the brethren have liberty to require satisfaction in a modest manner, concerning any publick breach of rule, as hath been mentioned above out of Acts 11. 2, 3, &c.

6. It

6. It belongeth to the *Elders*, to *prepare matters beforehand*, which are to bee transacted by themselves, or others, in the face of the Congregation, as the *Apostles* and *Elders* being met at the house of *James*, gave direction to *Paul* how to carry himselfe that hee might prevent the offence of the Church, when he should appeare before them, Act. 21.18. Hence when the offence of a brother is (according to the rule in *Matth.* 18,17.) to be brought to the *Church*, they are beforehand to confider and enquire whether the offence be really given or no, whether duly proved, and orderly proceeded in by the brethren, according to rule, and not duly fatisfied by the offender: left themselves and the Church, be openly cumbred with unneceffary and tedious agitations: but that all things transacted before the the Church, be carried along with moft expedition and beft edification. In which refpect they have power to reject caufless and diforderly complaints, as well as to propound and handle juft complaints before the congregation.

7. In the handling of an offence before the Church, the Elders have authority both *Jus dicere*, and *Sententiam ferre*; When the offence appeareth truly fcandalous; the Elders have power from God to informe the Church, what the *Law* (or *Rule* and *Will*) of *Chrift* is for the cenfure of fuch an offence: And when the Church difcernes the fame, and hath no juft exception againft it, but condefcendeth thereto, it is a further act of the Elders power, to *give fentence against the offender*. Both thefe acts of power in the Minifters of the Gofpel, are foretold by *Ezekiel*, Chap. 44. 23, 24. *They shall teach my people the difference between holy and prophane, and cause them to difcern between the uncleane and the cleane*. And in *controverfie they shall stand in judgment, and they shall judge it according to my judgment, &c.*

8. The Elders have power *to difmiffe the Church* with *a bleffing* in the name of the Lord, *Num.*6.23. to 26. *Heb.*7.7.

9. The Elders have received power to *charge* any of the people in *private*, that none of them live either *inordinately* without a calling, or *idlely* in their calling, or *fcandaloufly* in any fort, 2 *Theff.*3.6. and verf. 8.10,11,12. The Apoftles command argueth a power in the Elders to charge thefe duties upon the people effectually.

10. What power belongeth to the Elders in a *Synod*, is more fitly to be fpoken to in the *Chapter of Synods*.

11. In cafe the Church should fall away to blafphemy againft Chrift, and obftinate rejection and perfecution of the way of grace, and either no Synod to be hoped for, or no help by a Synod, the Elders

ders have power to *withdraw* (or *separate*) the *Disciples* from them, and to carry away the Ordinances with them, and therewithall sadly to denounce the just Judgement of God against them, *Acts* 19. 9. *Exod.* 33. 7. *Mark.* 6. 11. *Luke* 10 11. *Acts* 13. 46.

Obj. But if Elders have all this power to exercise all these acts of Rule, partly over the private members, partly over the whole Church, how are they then called the *servants of the Church?* 2 Cor. 4. 5.

Answ. The Elders to be both Servants and Rulers of the Church, may both of them stand well together. For their Rule is not lordly, as if they ruled of themselves, or for themselves, but stewardly and ministeriall, as ruling the Church from Christ, and also from their call: and withall, ruling the Church for Christ; and for the Church, even for their spirituall everlasting good. A Queen may call her servants, her Mariners, to pilot and conduct her over the Sea to such an Haven: yet they being called by her to such an office, shee must not rule them in steering their course, but must submit her self to be ruled by them, till they have brought her to her desired Haven. So is the case between the Church and her Elders.

CHAP. VI.
Of the Power and Authority *given to* Synods.

Synods wee acknowledge, being rightly ordered, as an Ordinance of Christ. Of their Assembly we find three just causes in Scripture. 1. When a Church wanting light or peace at home, desireth the counsell and help of other churches, few or moe. Thus the *Church of Antioch*, being annoyed with corrupt teachers, who darkned the light of the truth, and bred no small dissension amongst them in the church; they sent *Paul* and *Barnabas* and other *messengers* unto the *Apostles* and *Elders* at *Hierusalem*, for the establishment of Truth and Peace. In joyning the *Elders* to the *Apostles* (and that doubtlesse by the advice of *Paul* and *Barnabas*) it argueth that they sent not to the *Apostles* as extraordinary and infallible, and authenticall Oracles of God, (for then what need the advice and help of *Elders?*) but as wise and holy guides of the church, who might not only relieve them by some wise counsell, and holy order, but also set a precedent to succeeding ages, how errours and dissensions in churches might be removed and healed. And the course which the
Apostles

Apostles and Elders took for clearing the matter, was not by publishing the counsell of God with Apostolique authority, from immediate revelation, but by searching out the truth in an ordinary way of free disputation, *Acts* 15. ver. 7. which is as fit a course for imitation in after ages, as it was seasonable for practice then.

2. Just consequence from Scripture giveth us another ground for the assembly of many churches, or of their messengers, into a Synod, when any church lieth under scandall, through corruption in doctrine and practice, and will not be healed by more private advertisements of their owne members, or of their neighbour Ministers, or Brethren. For there is a brotherly communion, as between the members of the same church; so between the churches. *We have a little sister* (saith one church to another, *Cant.* 8. 8.) therefore churches have a brotherly communion amongst themselves. Looke then as one brother being offended with another, and not able to heal him by the mouth of two or three Brethren privately, it behooveth him to carry it to the whole church; so by proportion, if one church see matter of offence in another, and be not able to heal it in a more private way, it will behove them to procure the Assembly of many churches, that the offence may be orderly heard, and judged and removed.

3. It may so fall out, that the state of all the churches in the countrey may be corrupted; and beginning to discern their corruption, may desire the concurse and counsel of one another, for a speedy and safe, and generall reformation. And then so meeting and conferring together, may renew their covenant with God, and conclude and determine upon a course, that may tend to the publike healing, and salvation of them all. This was a frequent practice in the old Testament, in the time of *Asa*, 2 *Chron.* 15. 10. to 15. in the time of *Hezekiah*, 2 *Chron.* 29. 4. to 19. In the time of *Josiah*, 2 *Chron.* 34. 29. to 33. and in the time of *Ezra*, Ezra 10, 1. to 5. These and the like examples were not peculiar to the *Israelites*, as one intire *nationall Church*: For in that respect they appealed from every *Synagogue* and Court in *Israel*, to the *nationall high Priest*, and Court at *Jerusalem*, as being all of them subordinate thereunto (and therefore that precedent is usually waved by our best Divines, as not appliable to Christian churches:) but these examples hold forth no superioritie in one church or court over another, but all of them in an equall manner, give advice in common, and take one common course for redresse of all. And therefore such examples are fit precedents

for

for churches of equall power within themselves, to assemble together, and take order with one accord, for the reformation of them all).

Now a *Synod* being assembled, three questions arise about their power: 1. *What* is that *power* they have received? 2. How far the *fraternity concurreth* with the Presbyterie in it; the brotherhood with the Eldership? 3. Whether the power they have received reacheth to the injoyning of things, both in their nature, and in their use indifferent?

For the first; we dare not say that their power reacheth no farther then giving counsell: for such as their ends be, for which according to God, they do assemble, such is the power given them of God, as may attain those ends. As they meet to minister light and peace to such churches, as through want of light and peace lie in errour (or doubt at least) and variance; so they have power by the grace of Christ, not only to give light and counsell in matter of Truth and Practice; but also to command and injoyn the things to be believed and done. The expresse words of the Synodall letter imply no lesse, *It seemed good to the Holy Ghost, and unto us, to lay upon you no other burthen,* Acts 15. 27. This burthen therefore, to observe those necessary things which they speak of, they had power to impose. It is an act of the binding power of the keys, to *bind burthens*. And this *binding power* ariseth not only *materially* from the weight of the matters imposed, (which are necessary *necessitate præcepti* from the word) but also *formally*, from the authoritie of the Synod, which being an Ordinance of Christ, bindeth the more for the Synods sake. As a truth of the Gospel taught by a Minister of the Gospel, it bindeth to faith and obedience, not only because it is Gospel, but also because it is taught by a Minister for his callings sake, seeing Christ hath said, *Who so receiveth you receiveth mee.* And seeing also a Synod sometime meeteth to convince, and *admonish* an offending church or Presbyterie; they have power therefore, (if they cannot heal the offenders) to *determine to withdraw communion from them.* And further, seeing they meet likewise sometimes for generall reformation; they have power to *decree* and publish such *Ordinances*, as may conduce according to God, unto such reformation: Examples whereof we reade, Nehem. 10. 32. to 39. 2 *Chron.* 15. 12, 13.

For the second question; How far the *Fraternity*, or the *Brethren* of the church, may *concurre* with the *Elders* in exercising the power of the Synod?

The Answer is; The power which they have received, is a power of liberties. As 1. They have libertie to *dispute their doubts* modestly and Christianly among the *Elders*: For in that Synod at *Jerusalem*, as there was *much disputation*, Acts 15. 7. so the *multitude* had a part in the *Disputation*, v. 12. For after *Peters* Speech, it is said, *the whole multitude kept silence*, and silence from what? *to wit*, from the speech last in hand amongst them, and that was, from *Disputation*. 2. The *Brethren* of the church had libertie to joyn with the *Apostles* and *Elders*, in approving of the *sentence* of *Iames*, and determining the same as the common sentence of them all. 3. They had libertie to joyn with the *Apostles* and *Elders*, in *choosing* and *sending messengers*, and in *writing Synodall* Letters in the names of all, for the publishing of the sentence of the Synod. Both these points are expressed in the Text, v. 22. 23. to 29. Then pleased *it the Apostles and Elders, with the whole Church, to send chosen men, and to write Letters by them*. See the whole church distinguished from the *Apostles* and *Elders*; and those whom he called the *whole Church*, v. 22. hee calleth *the Brethren*, v. 23. *The Apostles, and Elders, and Brethren*, &c.

But though it may not be denied, that the *Brethren* of the church present in the Synod, had all this power of libertie, to joyn with the *Apostles* and *Elders* in all these acts of the Synod; yet the *authority of the Decrees* lay chiefly (if not only) in the *Apostles* and *Elders*. And therefore it is said, *Acts* 16. 4. *That Paul and Silas delivered to the churches for to keep the Decrees that were ordained of the Apostles and Elders:* So then it will be most safe to preserve to the Church of *Brethren* their due liberties, and to reserve to the *Elders* their due authority.

If it be said, The *Elders* assembled in a Synod, have no authority to determine or conclude any act that shall binde the churches, but according to the instructions which before they have received from the churches.

Answ. Wee do not so apprehend it; For what need churches send to a Synod for light and direction in wayes of truth and peace, if they be resolved afore-hand how far they will go? It is true, if the *Elders* of churches shall conclude in a Synod any thing prejudiciall to the Truth and Peace of the Gospel, they may justly expostulate with them at their return, and refuse such sanctions as the Lord hath not sancited. But if the *Elders* be gathered in the name of Christ in a Synod, and proceed according to the rule (the word) or Christ, they may consider and conclude sundry points expedient for the estate of their Churches, which the Churches were either ignorant or doubtfull of before.

As for the third question, Whether the Synod have power to injoyn such things as are both in their nature and their use indifferent? We should answer it negatively, and our reasons be:

1. From the pattern of that precedent of Synods, Acts 15. 28. They laid upon the Churches no *other burthen* but those *necessarie things*: necessary, though not all of them in their own nature, yet for present use, to *avoid the offence* both of *Jew* and *Gentile*: of the *Jew*, by *eating things strangled, and blood*; of the *Gentile* and *Jew* both, by *eating things sacrificed to Idols*, as *Paul* expoundeth that *Article* of the Synod, 1 Cor. 8, 10, 11, 12. and *Chap.* 10. 28. This eating with offence, was a murther of a weak brothers soule, & a sin against Christ, 1 *Cor.* 8. 11. 12. and therefore necessary to bee forborne, *necessitate præcepti*, by the necessity of Gods Commandement.

2. A second reason may be, from the latitude of the Apostolicall commission, which was given to them, *Mat.* 28. 19. 20. where the Apostles are commanded to *teach the people to observe all things which Christ had commanded*. If then the Apostles teach the people to observe more then Christ hath commanded, they goe beyond the bounds of their commission, and a larger commission then that given to the Apostles, nor Elders, nor Synods, nor Churches can challenge.

If it be said, Christ speaketh only of teaching such things which he had commanded as necessary to salvation.

Answ. If the Apostles or their successors should hereupon usurp an authority to teach the people things indifferent, they must plead this their authority from some other commission given them elsewhere: for in this place there is no foot-step for any such power. That much urged, and much abused place in 1 *Cor.* 14. 40. will not reach it: for though *Paul* requiring in that place, all the duties of Gods worship, whether Prayer, or Prophesying, or Psalmes, or Tongues, &c. that they should be performed *decently and orderly*, hee thereby forbiddeth any performance thereof undecently; as for men with long haire, and women to speak in open assemblies, especially to pray with their hair loose about them. And though he forbiddeth also men *speaking two or three at once*, which to do, were not *order*, but *confusion*; yet he doth not at all, neither himself injoyn, nor allow the Church of *Corinth* to injoyn such things as decent, whose want, or whose contrary is not undecent; nor such orders, whose want or contrary would be no disorder. Suppose the Church of Corinth, (or or any other Church or Synod) should enjoyn their Ministers to preach in a gown. A gown is a decent garment to preach in: yet such an Injunction is not grounded upon that Text of the Apostle. For then a Minister neglecting to preach in a gowne, should neglect the commandement of the Apostle, which yet indeed he doth not. For if hee preach in a cloak, hee preacheth decently enough, and that is all which the Apostles Canon reacheth to. In these things Christ never provided for *uniformity*, but onely for *unity*.

For a third reason of this point, (and to adde no more) it is taken from the nature of the Ministeriall Office, whether in a Church or Synod. Their office is *stewardly*, not *lordly*: they are Embassadours from Christ, and for Christ. Of a *Steward* it is required to be found faithfull, 1 *Cor*. 4. 1, 2. and therefore he may dispense no more injunctions to Gods house, then Christ hath appointed him: Neither may an Embassadour proceed to doe any act of his office, further then what he hath received in his Commission from his Prince. If he goe further, he maketh himselfe a Prævaricator, not an Embassadour.

But if it be enquired, *Whether a Synod hath power of Ordination and Excommunication*; we would not take upon us hastily to censure the many notable precedents of ancient and later Synods, who have put forth acts of power in both these kinds. Onely we doubt that *from the beginning it was not so*: And for our own parts, if any occasion of using this power should arise amongst our selves (which hitherto, through preventing mercie, it hath not) we (in a Synod) should rather chuse to *determine*, and to *publish* and *declare* our determination. That the ordination of such as we find fit for it, and the excommunication of such as we find doe deserve it, would be an acceptable service both to the Lord, and to his Churches: but the *administration* of both these acts we should refer to the *Presbytery* of the *severall Churches*, whereto the person to be ordained is called, and whereof the person to bee excommunicate is a member: and both acts to bee performed in the presence, and with the consent of the severall Churches, to whom the matter appertaineth For in the beginning of the Gospel in that precedent of Synods, Acts 15. we find the false teachers *declared* to be *disturbers* and *troublers* of the Churches, and *subverters of their soules*, Acts 15, 24. but no condigne censure dispensed against them by the Synod. An evident argument to us, that they left the censure of such offenders (in case they repented

pented not) to the particular Churches, to whom they did appertain. And for Synodicall ordination, although Acts 1. be alledged, where *Matthias* was called to be an Apostle, yet it doth not appear that they acted then in a Synodicall way, no more then the *Church of Antioch* did when with *fasting and prayer* they by their Presbyters *imposed hands* on *Paul* and *Barnabas*, and thereby *separated* them to *the work* of the Apostleship, whereto the *holy Ghost had called them*, Acts 13. 1, 2, 3. Whence as the holy Ghost then said, Ἀφορίσατε δέ μοι τόν τε Βαρνάβαν καὶ τὸν Σαῦλον: so thereupon *Paul* stileth himself Ἀπόστολος ἀφωρισμένος, Rom. 1. 1. And this was done in a particular Church, not in a Synod.

Chap. VII.

Touching the first Subject of all the forementioned power of the Keyes. And an explanation of Independency.

What that Church is, which is the first Subject of the power of the Keys, and whether this Church have an independent power in the exercise thereof, though they bee made two distinct Questions, yet (if candidly interpreted) they are but one. For whatsoever is the first Subject of any accident or adjunct, the same is independent in the enjoyment of it, that is, in respect of deriving it from any other subject like it self. As if fire be the first subject of heat, then it dependeth upon no other subject for heat. Now in the first subject of any power, three things concur. 1. It first receiveth that power whereof it is the first subject, and that reciprocally. 2. It first addeth and putteth forth the exercise of that power. 3. It first communicateth that power to others. As we see in fire, which is the first subject of heat: it first receiveth heat, and that reciprocally. All fire is hot, and whatsoever is hot is fire, or hath fire in it. Again, Fire first putteth forth heat it selfe, and also first communicateth heat to whatsoever things else are hot. To come then to the first subject of Church-power, or the power of the keyes. The substance of the doctrine thereof, may be conceived and declared in a few Propositions. Church-power is either *supream* and *soveraign*, or *subordinate* and *ministeriall*. Touching the former, take this proposition.

The Lord Jesus *Christ*, the *head* of his Church, is the Πρῶτον Δεκτικόν, the first proper subject of the *soveraigne power* of the Keyes. *He hath the Key of David: He openeth, and no man shutteth; He shutteth, and no man openeth*, Rev. 3. 7. *The government is upon his shoulders*, Isa. 9. 6. And himself declareth the same to his Apostles, as the ground of his granting to them Apostolicall power. *All power* (saith he) *is given to me in heaven and earth*, Matth. 28. 18. *Go therefore, &c.*

Hence 1. *All legislative power* (power of making Lawes) in the Church, is in him, and not from him derived to any other, *Jam*. 4. 12 *Isa.* 33. 22. The power derived to others, is onely to publish and execute his Lawes and Ordinances, and to see them observed, *Mat.* 28. 20. *His Laws are perfect*, Psal. 19. 9. and doe *make the man of God perfect* to every *good worke*, 2 Tim. 3. 17. and need no addition.

2. From his soveraigne power it proceedeth, that he onely can erect and ordain a true constitution of a Church estate, *Hebr.* 3. 3. to 6. *He buildeth his own house*, and setteth the patterne of it, as God gave to *David* the patterne of *Salomons* Temple, 1 *Chron.* 28. 19. None hath power to erect any other Church-frame, then as this Master-builder hath left us a pattern thereof in the Gospel. In the old Testament, the *Church* set up by him, was *Nationall*, in the New, *Congregationall*; Yet so as that in sundry cases it is ordered by him, many Congregations or their Messengers, may bee assembled into a Synod, *Acts* 15.

3. It is from the same soveraigne power, that all the offices, or ministeries in the Church, are ordained by him, 1 *Cor.* 12. 5. yea and all the *members are set in the body by him*, together with all the power belonging to their offices and places: as in the naturall body, so in the Church, 1 *Cor.* 12. 18.

4. From this soveraign power in like sort It is, that all gifts to discharge any office, by the officers, or any duty by the members, are from him, 1 *Cor.* 12. 11. All *treasures of wisdome*, and knowledge, and grace, and the fulnesse thereof, are in him for that end, *Col.* 2. 3. and v. 9. 10. *Joh.* 1. 16.

From this soveraigne power it is, that all the spirituall power, and efficacie, and blessing, in the administration of these gifts in these offices and places, for the gathering and edifying, and perfecting of all the Churches, and of all the Saints in them, is from him, *Mat.* 28. 20. *Lo, I am with you alwayes, &c.* Col. 1. 29, 1 Cor. 15. 9.

The good pleasure of the Father, the personall union of the humane nature with the eternall Son of God, his purchase of his Church with his own blood, and his deep humiliation of himselfe unto the death of the Crosse, have all of them obtained to him this his highest exaltation, to be *head over all things unto the Church*, and to

injoy

injoy as king thereof this soveraigne power, *Col.* 1. 19. *Col.* 2. 2, 9, 10. *Act.* 20. 28. *Phil.* 2. 8. to 11.

But of this soveraign power of Christ, there is no question amongst *Protestants*, especially studious of Reformation. Now as concerning the *Ministeriall* power, wee give these following *Propositions*.

I. *Propos.* A particular *Church or congregation of Saints, professing the faith,* TAKEN INDEPENDENTLY FOR ANY CHURCH (one as well as another) *is the first subject of all the Church-offices, with all their spirituall gifts and power,* which Christ hath given to be executed amongst them; *whether it be* Paul, *or* Apollos, *or* Cephas, *all are yours,* (speaking to the Church of *Corinth,* 1 *Cor.* 3. 22.) not as a peculiar priviledge unto them, but common to them, with any other particular church; And theirs was such a church, of whom it is said, *That they came all together into one place,* for the communication of their spirituall gifts, 1 *Cor.* 14. 23. And *Paul* telleth the same church, that *God hath set the officers,* and their gifts, and all varietie of members, and their Functions *in his Church,* 1 *Cor.* 14. 28. where it is not so well translated [*Some*] God hath *set some* in his church; for he hath set all; but speaking of the members of the church, *v.* 27. he proceedeth to exemplifie those members, in *v.* 28. ὓς μὲν ἔθετο Θεὸς ἐν τῇ ἐκκλησίᾳ *and which God hath set in his Church*; that is, which members, *Apostles Prophets, &c.* For though the Relative be not of the same gender with the Antecedent before, yet it is an usuall thing with the Pen-men of the new Testament, to respect the sense of the words, and so the person intended, rather then the gender of their name, and to render the Relative of the same gender and case with the Substantive following: so here ὓς μὲν Ἀποστόλους, Προφήτας, &c.

In the new Testament, it is not a new observation that wee never reade of any nationall church, nor of any nationall officers given to them by Christ. In the old Testament indeed, wee reade of a Nationall church. All the tribes of *Israel* were three times in a yeere to appeare before the Lord in *Jerusalem,* Deut. 16. 16. And he appointed them there an high Priest of the whole nation, and certain solemne sacrifices by him to be administred, *Lev.* 16. 1. to 29. and together with him other Priests and Elders, and Judges, to whom all appeals should be brought, and who should judge all difficult and transcendent cases, *Deut.* 17. 8. to 11. but wee reade of no such nationall church or high Priest, or court in the new Testament; And yet wee willingly grant that particular churches of equall power, may

may in some cases appointed by Christ, meet together by themselves, or by their messengers in a Synod, and may perform sundry acts of power there, as hath been shewed above. But the officers themselves, and all the Brethren members of the Synod; yea, and the Synods themselves, and all the power they put forth, they are all of them *primarily* given to the severall churches of particular Congregations, either as the first subject in whom they are resident, or as the first object about whom they are conversant, and for whose sake they are gathered and imployed.

11. *Propos.* *The Apostles of Christ were the first subject of Apostolicall power;* Apostolicall power stood chiefly in two things: First, in that each Apostle had in him all ministeriall power of all the officers of the Church. They by vertue of their office, might *exhort as Pastors,* 1 Tim. 2. 1. *teach as Teachers,* 1 Tim. 2. 7. *rule as Rulers,* 2 Tim. 4. 1. *receive,* and *distribute* the oblations of the churches as *Deacons,* Act. 4. 35. yea, any one Apostle or Euangelist carried about with him the libertie and power of the whole church; and therefore might *baptize*; yea, and censure an offender too, as if hee had the presence and concurrence of the whole Church with him. For wee reade that *Philip* baptized the Eunuch without the presence of any church, *Acts* 8. 38. And that *Paul* himself excommunicated *Alexander,* 1 Tim. 1. 20. and it is not mentioned that hee took the consent of any Church or Presbyterie in it. It is true indeed, where he could have the consent and concurse of the Church and Presbyterie in exercise of any act of church-power, hee willingly took it, and joyned with it, as in the ordination of *Timothy* (2 Tim. 1. 6. with 1 Tim. 4. 14.) and in the excommunication of the incestuous *Corinthian,* 1 Cor. 5. 4, 5. But when both himself and the person to be baptized, or ordained, or excommunicated, were absent and distant from all churches, the Apostles might proceed to put forth their power in the administration of any church act without them. The multitude and plenitude of power, which they received immediately from Christ, would beare them out in it. *As my Father sent mee* (saith Christ) *to wit,* with amplitude and plenitude of soveraign power, *so send I you* (with like amplitude and plenitude of ministeriall power) *Ioh.* 20. 21.

2. Apostolicall power extended it self to all churches, as much as to any one. *Their line went out into all the world,* (Psal. 19. 4. compared with *Rom.* 10.) And as they received commission to preach and baptize

baptize in all the world, *Mat.* 28. 19. So they received charge to *feed* the flock of Christs *Sheep and Lambs* (which implyeth all acts of Pastorall government over all the *Sheep* and *Lambs* of Christ) *Joh.* 21. 15, 16, 17. Now this Apostolicall power, centring all church-power into one man, and extending it self forth to the circumference of all churches, as the Apostles were the first subject of it, so were they also the last; Neverthelesse, that ample and universall latitude of power, which was conjoyned in them, is now divided even by themselves amongst all the churches, and all the officers of the churches respectively, the officers of each church attending the charge of the particular church committed to them, by vertue of their office, and yet none of them neglecting the good of other churches, so far as they may be mutually helpfull to one another in the Lord.

III. *Propof.* When the church of a particular congregation walketh together in the truth and peace, the *Brethren* of the church are the *first subject of church-liberty*, and the *Elders* thereof of *church-authority*, and *both* of them together are the first subject of *all church-power* needfull to be exercised within themselves, whether in the election and ordination of officers, or in the censure of offenders in their own body.

Of this *Proposition* there be three *Branches*: 1. That the Brethren of a particular church of a Congregation, are the first subjects of church-liberty: 2. That the Elders of a particular church, are the first subjects of church-authoritie: 3. That both the Elders and Brethren, walking and joyning together in truth and peace, are the first subjects of all church-power, needfull to be exercised in their own body.

Now that the key of church-priviledge or libertie is given to the Brethren of the church, and the key of rule and authority to the Elders of the church, hath been declared above, in *Chapt.* 3. But that these are the first subjects of these keys; and first the church, the first subject of liberty, may appeare thus.

From the removall of any former subject of this power or liberty, from whence they might derive it. If the Brethren of the Congregation were not the first subject of their church-libertie, then they derived it either from their own Elders, or from other Churches. But they derived it not from their own Elders: for they had power and liberty to choose their own Elders, as hath been shewed above, and therefore they had this liberty before they had Elders, and so could not derive it from them.

Nor did they derive it from other particular churches. For all particular churches are of equall liberty and power within themselves, not one of them subordinate to another. Wee reade not in Scripture, that the Church of *Corinth* was subject to that of *Ephesus*, not that of *Ephesus* to *Corinth*; no, nor that of *Cenchrea* to *Corinth*, though it was a church situate in their vicinity.

Nor did they derive their libertie from a Synod of churches. For we found no foot-step in the pattern of Synods, *Acts* 15. that the Church of *Antioch* borrowed any of their liberties from the Synod at *Jerusalem*. They borrowed indeed light from them, and decrees, tending to the establishment of truth and peace. For upon the publishing of the decrees of that Synod, the Churches were established in the faith (or truth) *Act.* 16. 4, 5. and also in consolation and peace, *Act.* 15. 31, 32. but they did not borrow from them any church-liberty at all.

2. Now, the *second branch* of the *Proposition* was, That the Elders of the church of a particular Congregation, are the first subject of rule or authoritie, in that church (or congregation) over which the Holy Ghost hath made them over-seers.

1. From the charge of rule over the Church committed to them immediately from Christ: For though the Elders be chosen to their office by the church of Brethren, yet the office it selfe is ordained immediatly by Christ, and the rule annexed to the office, is limited by Christ onely. If the Brethren of the church should elect a presbyterie to be called by them in the Lord, this will not excuse the Presbyters in their neglect of rule, either before the Lord, or to their own consciences. For thus runneth the Apostles charge to the Elders of *Ephesus*, (Act. 20. 28.) *Take heed to your selves, and to the whole flock, over which the Holy Ghost hath made you over-seers.*

2. The same appeareth from the gift of rule, required especially in an Elder, without which they are not capable of election to that office in the church, 1 *Tim.* 3, 4, 5. He must be one *that is able to rule well his own house*, or else how shall he order the church of God? The like gift of rule is not necessary to the admission of a member into the church, as to the election of an Elder: If a private brother be not so well able (through weaknesse in prudence or courage) to rule his own house, it will not justly debarre him from entrance into the church; but the like defect will justly debar a man from election to the office of an Elder. Neither hath God given a spirit of

rule

rule and government ordinarily to the greater part of the body of the brethren: and therefore neither hath he given them the first Receit of the key of Authoritie, to whom he hath not given the gift to employ it.

If it be objected; How can the brethren of the Church invest an Elder with rule over them, if they had not power of rule in themselves to communicate to him?

Ans. They invest him with rule, partly by chusing him to the office which God hath invested with rule, partly by professing their own subjection to him in the Lord: wee by the rule of Relatives doe necessarily inferre, and preferre the authoritie of the Elders over them. For in yeelding subjection, they either set up, or acknowledge Authoritie in him, to whom they yeeld subjection.

Ob. 2. The body of the Church is the Spouse of Christ, the Lambs wife, and ought not the wife to rule the servants and stewards in the house, rather then they her? Is it not meet that the keyes of Authoritie should hang at her girdle rather then at theirs?

Answ. There is a difference to be put between Queenes, Princesses, Ladies of great Honour, (such as the Church is to Christ, *Psal.* 45. 9.) and Countrey huswives, poore mens wives. Queenes and great persons have severall offices and officers for every businesse and service about the house, as Chamberlains, Stewards, Treasurers, Comptrollers, Ushers, Bayliffs, Groomes, and Porters, who have all the authoritie of ordering the affaires of their Lords house in their hands. There is not a key left in the Queens hand of any office, but onely of power and libertie to call for what she wanteth according to the Kings royall allowance: which if she exceed, the officers have power to restrain her by order from the King. But countrey huswives, and poore mens wives, whose husbands have no Officers, Bayliffs or Stewards, to oversee and order their estates, they may carry the keyes of any office at their own girdles, which the husband keepeth not in his own hand. Not because poore huswives have greater authoritie in the house then Queens; but because of their poverty and mean estate, they are fain to be in stead of many servants to their husbands.

Obj. 3. The whole body naturall, is the first subject of all the naturall power of any member in the body; as the facultie of sight is first in the body, before in the eye.

Answ. It is not in the mysticall body (the Church) in all respects alike, as in the naturall body. In the naturall body there be all the faculties of each part actually inexistent, though not exerting or putting forth themselves, till each member be articulated and formed. But in the body of the Church of Brethren it is not so. All the severall functions of Church-power, are not actually inexistent in the body of Brethren, unlesse some of them have the gifts of all the Officers, which often they have not, having neither Presbyters, nor men fit to be Presbyters. Now if the power of the Presbytery were given to a particular Church of Brethren, as such, *primo & per se*, then it would be found in every particular Church of Brethren. For *à quatenus ad omnia valet consequentia.*

Obj. 4. But it is an usuall tenent in many of our best Divines, that the government of the Church is mixt of a Monarchy, an Aristocracie, and a Democracy. In regard of Christ the head, the government of the Church is soveraigne and monarchicall. In regard of the Rule by the Presbytery, it is stewardly and Aristocraticall: in regard of the peoples power in elections and censures, it is Democraticall: which argueth, the people have some stock of κράτος, power and authoritie in the government of the Church.

Answ. In a large sense, Authority after a sort, may be acknowledged in the people. As 1. when a man acteth by counsell according to his own discerning freely, he is then said to be αὐτεξούσιος, *Dominus sui actus.* So the people in all the acts of liberty which they put forth are *Domini sui actus*, Lords of their own action.

2. The people by their acts of liberty, as in election of Officers, and concurrency in censure of offenders, and in the Determination and Promulgation of Synodall acts; they have a great stroke or power in the ordering of Church-affairs, which may be called κράτος, or *potestas*, a Power, which many times goeth under the name of rule or authoritie, but in proper speech it is rather a priviledge or libertie then authoritie, as hath been opened above in *Chap.* 3. For no act of the peoples power or liberty doth properly bind, unlesse the authoritie of the Presbytery concurre with it.

3. A third argument whereby it may appeare, that the Elders of a particular Church are the first subject of authoritie in that Church, is taken from the like removall of other subjects, from whence they might be thought to derive their authoritie, as was used before to prove the Church of Brethren was the first subject of their own libertie in their own Congregation. The Elders of Churches are never found in Scripture to derive their authority which they exercise in their own Congregation, either from the Elders of other Churches,

ches, or from any Synod or Churches. All particular Churches and all the Elders of them, are of equall power, each of them respectively in their owne congregations. None of them call others their Rabbies, or Masters, or Fathers (in respect of any authority over them) but all of them own and acknowledge one another as fellow-brethren, *Matth.* 23. 8, 9, 10.

And though in a Synod they have received power from Christ, and from his presence in the Synod, to exercise authority in imposing burthens (such as the holy Ghost laieth) upon all Churches whose Elders are present with them, *Acts* 15. 28. (for the Apostles were Elders in all Churches) yet the Elders of every particular Church, when they walk with the brethren of their own Church in light and peace, they need not to derive from the Synod any power to impose the same, or the like burthens, upon their owne Churches. For they have received a power and charge from Christ, to teach and command with all authority the whole counsel of God unto their people. And the people discerning the light of the truth delivered, and walking in peace with their Elders, they readily yeeld obedience to their Over-seers, in whatsoever they see and heare by them commended to them from the Lord.

3. Now wee come to the *third branch* of the third Proposition, which was this, That the Church of a particular congregation, Elders and Brethren walking and joyning together in truth and peace, are the first subject of all Church-power, needfull to bee exercised within themselves, whether in the election or ordination of officers, or in the censure of offenders in their own body.

The truth hereof may appeare by these Arguments. 1. In point of *Ordination*. From the compleat integrity of a Ministers calling (even to the satisfaction of his owne and the peoples conscience) when both the Brethren and the Elders of the particular Church whereto he is called, have put forth the power which belongeth to them about him. As, when the brethren of the Church have chosen him to office, and the Presbytery of the Church have laied their hands upon him: and both of them in their severall acts have due respect to the inward ministeriall gifts whereunto God hath furnished him: he may then looke at himself as called by the holy Ghost, to exercise his talents in that office amongst them, and the people may and ought to receive him, as sent of God to them.

What defect may be found in such a call, when the brethren exercise their lawfull liberty, and the Elders their lawfull authority, in his ordination, and nothing more is required to the compleat integrity of a Ministers calling? If it be said, there wanted imposition of hands by the Bishop, who succeeded in the place of *Timothy* and *Titus*, whom the Apostle *Paul* left, the one in Ephesus, the other in Crete, to ordain Elders in many Churches, *Tit.* 1. 5.

Answ. Touching ordination by *Timothy* and *Titus*, and (upon pretence of them) by Bishops, enough hath been said by many godly learned heretofore, especially of later times.

The summe commeth to these conclusions. 1. That *Timothy* and *Titus* did not ordain Elders in many Churches, as Bishops, but as Evangelists. *Timothy* is expresly termed an Evangelist, 2 *Tim.* 4. 5. And *Titus* is as clearly decyphered to be an Evangelist as *Timothy*, by the characters of an Evangelist, which either Scripture holdeth forth, or *Eusebius* noteth in his *Ecclesiast. Histor. lib.* 3. *cap.* 37. *Gr. cap.* 31. *Lat.* Not to be limited to a certain Church, but to follow the Apostles, finishing their work in planting and watering Churches where they came. They did indeed ordain officers where they wanted, and exercised jurisdiction (as the Apostles did) in severall Churches; yet with the rest of the Presbytery, and in the presence of the whole Church, 1. *Tim* 5. But for the continuance of this office of an Evangelist in the Church, there is no direction in the Epistles either to *Timothy* or *Titus*, or any where else in Scripture.

2. *Conclusion.* Those Bishops whose callings or offices in the Church, are set forth in those Epistles to be continued; they are altogether Synonyma with Presbyters, *Tit.* 1. 5. 7. 1 *Tim.* 3. 1. to 7.

3. *Conclus.* We read of many Bishops to one Church, *Phil.* 1. 1. *Act.* 14. 23. and Chap. 20. 17, 28. *Tit.* 1. 5. 7. but not of many Churches (much lesse all the Churches in a large Diocess) to one Bishop.

4. *Conclus.* There is no transcendent proper work, cut out, or reserved for such a transcendent officer as a Diocesan Bishop throughout the New Testament. The transcendent acts reserved to him by the Advocates of Episcopacie, are Ordination and Iurisdiction. Now both these are acts of Rule. And *Paul* to *Timothy* acknowledgeth no Rulers in the Church above Pastors and Teachers, who labour in word and doctrine, but rather Pastors and Teachers above them. The Elders (saith he) that rule well, are worthy of double honour, but especially they that labour in Word and Doctrine, 1. *Tim.* 5. 17.

5. *Conclus.* When after the Apostles times, one of the Pastors by way

way of eminencie was called Bishop for order sake, yet for many yeares he did no act of power, but 1. With consent of the Presbyterie. 2. With consent, and in the presence of the people. As is noted out of *Eusebius, Ecclesiast. Histor. lib. 6. cap. 43. Gr. ca. 35. Lat. Cyprian Epist. lib. 3. Epist. 10. & lib. 1. Epist. 3. Casaub. adversus Baronium; exercitat. 15. num. 28.*

When it is alledged out of *Hierome* to confirm the same, that in the primitive times, *Communi Presbyterorum consilio, Ecclesiæ gubernabantur.* It is a weake and poore evasion, to put it off with observing, that he saith, *Communi Presbyterorum consilio,* not *authoritate.* For 1. No authoritie is due to Presbyters over the Bishop or Pastor, no more then to the Pastor over them. They are συμπρεσβύτεροι, fellow-Elders, and coequall in authoritie. And 2. when *Hierome* saith, The Churches were governed by the common counsell of them all; It argueth, nothing was done against their counsell, but all with it, else it might be said, the Bishop governed the Churches with the common counsell of Presbyters, to wit, asked, but not followed. And that would imply a contradiction to *Hieromes* testimony, to say the Churches were governed by the sole authoritie of Bishops, and yet not without asking the common counsell of the Presbyters. For in asking their counsell, and not following it, the Bishop should order and governe the Churches against their counsell. Now that the churches were governed by the common counsell of Presbyters, and against the common counsell of Presbyters, are flat contradictories.

4. For a second Argument, to prove that the Brethren of the Church of a particular congregation, walking with their Elders in truth and peace, are the first subject of all that church-power which is needfull to be exercised in their own body: It is taken

From their indispensable and independent power in church censures. The censure that is ratified in heaven cannot be dispensed withall, nor reversed by any power on earth. Now the censure that is administred by the Church of a particular congregation, is ratified in Heaven. For so saith the Lord Jesus touching the power of Church-censures, *Matth.* 18. 17, 18. *If the offender refuse to heare the Church, let him be to thee as a Heathen and a Publican. Verily I say unto you, Whatsoever ye shall bind on earth, shall be bound in Heaven: and whatsoever yee shall loose on earth, shall be loosed in Heaven.*

Against this Argument from this Text many objections are wont to be made, but none that will hold.

Obj.

Object. 1. By *Church* in *Mat.* 18. 17. is not meant the Christian Church (for it was not yet extant, nor could the Apostles then have understood Christ if he had so meant) but the *Jewish* church, and so he delivereth their censure, in a *Jewish* phrase; to account a man as *an Heathen and a Publican.*

Answ. 1. The Christian Church, though it was not then extant, yet the Apostles knew as well what he meant by *Church* in *Mat.* 18. 17. as they understood what he meant by *building his Church upon the Rock* in *Mat.* 16. 18. It was enough the Apostles looked for a Church which Christ would gather, and build upon the confession of *Peters* faith; and being built, should be indued with heavenly power in their censures, which they more fully understood afterwards, when having received the Holy Ghost, they came to put these things in practice.

Answ. 2. The allusion in the Church-censure to the *Jewish* custome, in accounting a man as an *Heathen* and *Publican*, doth not argue that Christ directeth his Disciples to complaine of scandals to the *Jewish* Synagogues; but onely directeth them how to walk towards obstinate offenders, excommunicate by the Christian church, to wit, to walk towards them, as the *Jewes* walk towards *Heathens*, (to wit, denying to them religious communion) and as towards *Publicans*, with-holding from them familiar civill communion; for so the *Jews* said to Christs Disciples, *Why eateth your Master with Publicans and Sinners?*

Answ. 3. It is not credible, that Christ would send his Disciples to make complaint of their offences to the *Jewish* Synagogues:

For, first, Is it likely he would send his Lambs and Sheep, for right and healing, unto Wolves and Tigres? Both their Sanhedrim, and most of their Synagogues were no better. And if here and there some Elders of their Synagogues were better affected, yet how may it appear that so it was, where any of themselves dwelt? And if that might appear too, yet had not the *Jewes* already agreed; *That if any man did confesse Christ, he should be cast out of the Synagogues,* Joh. 9. 22.

Object. 2. Against the Argument from this Text, it is objected; That by the Church is meant the Bishop, or his Commissary.

Answ. 1. One man is not the Church.

If it be said, one man may represent a church; the reply is ready: one man cannot represent the Church, unlesse he be sent forth by the Church; but so is neither the Bishop nor his Commissary. They
send

and the power thereof. 41

send not for them, but they come unsent for, (like water into a Ship) chiefly for the terror of the servants of Christ, and for the incouragement of the prophane. And though some of Christs servants have found some favour from some few of Bishops, (men of more learning and ingenuity) yet those Bishops have found the lesse favour themselves from their fellow-Bishops.

Ans. 2. The Bishop ordinarily is no member of the Church of that congregation, where the offence is committed, and what is his satisfaction to the removall of the offence given to the Church?

Answ. 3. The new Testament acknowledgeth no such ruler in the Church, as claimeth honour above the Elders that labour in word and Doctrine, 1 *Tim.* 5. 17.

Object. 3. To tell the Church, is to tell the Presbyterie of the Church.

Answ. 1. We deny not, The offence is to be told to the Presbyterie; yet not to them as the Church, but as the guides of the church, who, if upon hearing the cause, and examining the witnesses, they find it right for publick censure, they are then to propound it to the Church, and to try and clear the state of the cause before the church, that so the church discerning fully the nature and quality of the offence, may consent to the judgement and sentence of the Elders against it, to the confusion of the offender; and the publick edification of them all, who hearing and fearing, will learn to beware of the like wickednesse.

Answ. 2. The Church is never put for the Presbyterie alone (throughout the new Testament) though sometime it be put expresly for the Fraternity alone, as they are distinguished from the Elders and Officers, *Act.* 15. 22. and therefore Tell the Church, cannot be meant Tell the Presbyterie alone.

Object. In the old Testament, the Congregation is often put for the Elders and Rulers of the Congregation.

Answ. Let all the places alledged be examined, and it will appear, that in matters of judgement, where the Congregation is put for the Elders and Rulers, it is never meant (for ought we can find) of the Elders and Rulers alone, sitting apart, and retired from the Congregation; but sitting in the presence of the Congregation, and hearing and judging causes before them: In which case, if a sentence have passed from a Ruler, with the dislike of the Congregation, they have not stuck to shew their dislike, sometime by protesting openly against it (as 1 *Sam.* 14. 44, 45.) sometime by refusing

fusing to execute it. (1 *Sam.* 20. 16, 17.) And what the people of the Congregation lawfully did in some cases, at some times, in waving and counterpoizing the sentence of their Rulers, the same they might and ought to have done in the like cases at any time. The whole Host or Congregation of *Israel* might protest against an unrighteous illegall sentence; and a part of the Congregation, who discerned the iniquity of a sentence, might justly withdraw themselves from the execution of it.

Obj. 4. When Christ said *Tell the Church,* he meant a Synodicall or Classicall Assembly of the Presbyters of many Churches. For it was his meaning and purpose in this place, to prescribe a rule for the removing of all scandals out of the Church, which cannot be done by telling the Church of one Congregation; for what if an Elder offend; yea, what if the whole Presbytery offend? The people or brethren have not power to judge their Judges, to rule their Rulers. Yea, what if the whole Congregation fall under an offence (as they may do, *Lev.* 4. 13.) a Synod of many Presbyters may reform them, but so cannot any one Congregation alone; if the Congregation that gave the offence stand out in it.

Answ. 1. Reserving due honour to Synods rightly ordered, or (which is all one) a *Classis* or *Convention* of Presbyters of particular churches, we do not find that a Church is any where put for a Synod of Presbyteries. And it were very incongruous in this place: For though it be said a particular Congregation cannot reach the removall of all offences; so it may be as truly said, that it were unmeet to trouble Synods with every offence that falleth out in a Congregation; Offences fall out often, Synods meet but seldome; and when they do meet, they find many more weightie imployments, then to attend to every offence of every private brother. Besides, as an whole particular Congregation may offend, so may a generall Assembly of all the Presbyters in a Nation offend also: For generall Councels have erred; and what remedie shall be found to remove such errors and offences out of this Text? Moreover, if an offence be found in a Brother of a Congregation, and the Congregation be found faithfull and willing to remove it by due censure; why should the offence be called up to a more publick Judicature, and the plaister made broader then the sore?

Again, If an Elder offend, the rest of the Presbyterie with the Congregation joyning together, may proceed against him, (if they cannot otherwise heal him) and so remove the offence from amongst them.

them. If the whole Presbyterie offend, or such a part as will draw a party and a faction in the Church with them, their readiest course is, to bring the matter then to a Synod. For though this place in *Matthew* direct not to that; yet the holy Ghost leaveth us not without direction in such a case, but giveth us a pattern in the church of *Antioch*, to repair to a Synod. And the like course is to be taken in the offence of a whole Congregation, if it be persisted in with obstinacy. Neither is it true which was said, that it was the purpose of Christ in *Matth.* 18. 17. to prescribe a rule for the removall of all offences out of the Church; but onely of such private and lesse hainous offences, as grow publick and notorious onely by obstinacy of the offenders: For if offences be hainous and publick at first, the holy Ghost doth not direct us to proceed in such a generall course from a private admonition by one brother alone, and then to a second, by one or two more, and at last, to tell it to the Church. But in such a case the Apostle giveth another rule, (1 *Corinth.* 5. 11.) to cast an hainous notorious offender, both out of church-communion, and private familiar communion also.

Object. 5. The Church here spoken of, *Matth.* 18. 17. is such an one, as whereto a complaint may orderly be made: But a complaint cannot be orderly made to a multitude, such as an whole Congregation is.

Answ. And why may not a complaint be orderly made to a whole multitude? The *Levite* made an orderly complaint to a greater multitude, then 400. particular Congregations are wont to amount to, *Jud.* 20. 1, 2, 3, 4, &c.

Object. 6. The Church here to be complained of meeteth with authority, (for censures are administred with authority) but the church of a particular Congregation meeteth with humility, to seek the face and favour of God.

Answ. Humility to God may well stand with authority to men. The 24. Elders (who represent the growne heyres of the Church of the new Testament) they are said in Church-assemblies to sit upon thrones with crowns on their heads, *Revel.* 4. 4. yet when they fall down to worship God and the Lamb, they cast down their crowns at his feet, *v.* 10.

Object. 7. In the church of a particular Congregation, a woman may not speak: but in this Church here spoken of, they may speak; for they may be offenders, and offenders must give an account of their offences.

G 2 [*Answ.* When

Ans. When the Apostle forbiddeth women to speak in the church, he meaneth, speaking partly by way of authority, as in publick praying or prophesying in the Church, (1 *Tim.* 2. 12.) partly by way of bold inquiry, in asking questions publickly of the Prophets in the face of the Church, 1 *Cor.* 14. 34. But to answer it: If the whole Congregation have taken just offence at the open sin of a woman, she is bound as much to give satisfaction to the whole Congregation, as well as to the Presbyterie.

Object. 8. When Schismes grew to be scandalous in the Church of *Corinth*, the houshold of *Chloe* told not the whole Congregation of it, but *Paul*, 1 Cor. 1. 11.

Answ. The contentions in the Church of *Corinth* were not the offence of a private brother, but of the whole church. And who can tell whether they had not spoken of it to the Church before? But whether they had or no, the example onely argueth, that Brethren offended with the sins of their brethren, may tell an Elder of the Church of it, that he may tell it to the Church, which no man denieth. *Paul* was an Elder of every church of Christ, as the other Apostles were, as having the government of all the churches committed to them all.

Having thus (by the help of Christ) cleared this Text in *Mat.* 18: 17. from varietie of misconstructions, (which not the obscurity of the words, but the eminency of the gifts, and worth of Expositors hath made difficult) Let us adde an argument or two more to the same purpose, to prove, that the Church of a particular Congregation, fully furnished with officers, and rightly walking in judgement and peace, is the first subject of all Church-authority, needfull to be exercised within their own body.

3. A third argument to prove this, is usually and justly taken from the practice and example of the Church of *Corinth*, in the excommunication of the incestuous *Corinthian*, 1 Cor. 5. 1. to 5.

Obj. 1. The excommunication of the incestuous *Corinthian*, was not an act of judiciall authority in the church of *Corinth*, whether Elders or Brethren, but rather an act of subjection to the Apostle, publishing the sentence, which the Apostle had before decreed and judged: for (saith the Apostle) I though absent in body, yet present in spirit, have judged already, concerning him that hath done this deed, &c.

Answ. 1. Though *Paul* (as a chiefe Officer of every church) judged before-hand the excommunication of the incestuous *Corin-*

thian? yet his judgement was not a judiciall sentence, delivering him to Satan, but a judicious doctrine and instruction, teaching the Church what they ought to do in that case.

2. The act of the church in *Corinth* in censuring the incestuous person, was indeed an act of subjection to the Apostles divine doctrine and direction (as all church-censures, by whomsoever administred, ought to be acts of subjection to the word of Christ) but yet their act was a compleat act of just power, (even an act of all that liberty and authority which is to be put forth in any censure.) For, first they delivered him to Satan, in the name of the Lord Jesus, and with the power of the Lord Jesus, *v.* 4. and that is the highest power in the Church. Secondly, the spirit of *Paul*, that is, his Apostolike spirit was gathered together with them, in delivering and publishing the sentence; which argueth, both his power and theirs was co-incident and concurrent in this sentence. Thirdly, the holy end and use of this sentence argueth the heavenly power from whence it proceeded. They delivered him to Satan for the destruction of the flesh (that is, for the mortifying of his corruption) that his soul might be saved in the day of the Lord Jesus. Fourthly, when his soul came to be humble and penitent by the means of this sentence, *Paul* intreateth the church to release and forgive him, 2 Cor. 2. 6. to 10. Now *ejusdem potestatis est ligare & solvere, claudere & aperire.*

Object. 2. All this argueth no more, but that some in the church of *Corinth* had this power (to wit, the Presbytery of the church, but not the whole body of the people) to excommunicate the offender.

Answ. 1. If the Presbyterie alone had put forth this power, yet that sufficeth to make good the Proposition, that every church furnished with a Presbyterie, and proceeding righteously and peaceably, they have within themselves so much power as is requisite, to be exercised within their own body.

Answ. 2. It is apparent by the Text, that the Brethren concurred also in this sentence, and that with *some act of power*, to wit, such power as the want of putting it forth, retarded the sentence, and the putting of it forth was requisite to the administration of the sentence.

For, first, the reproofe for not proceeding to sentence sooner, is directed to the whole church, as well as to the Presbyterie; *They are all blamed for not mourning, for not putting him away, for being* u *ffed up rather,* 1 Cor. 5. 2.

2. The commandment is directed to them all, *when they are gathered together*, (and what is that but to a Church meeting?) to proceed against him, 1 *Cor*. 5. 4. In like sort, in the end of the Chapter he commandeth them all, *Put away therefore from among you that wicked person*, v. 13.

3. He declareth this act of theirs in putting him out, to be a judiciall act, *v*.12. *Do you not judge them that are within?* Say that the judgement of authoritie be proper onely to the Presbytery, yet the judgement of discretion (which as concurring in this act with the Presbytery,) hath a power in it (as was said) may not be denied to the Brethren: for here is an act of judgement ascribed to them all: which judgement in the Brethren he esteemeth of it so highly, that from thence he taketh occasion to advise the members of the Church, to refer their differences even in civill matters, to the judgement of the Saints or Brethren. *Know ye not* (saith he) that *the Saints shall judge the world? yea the Angels?* 1 Cor. 6. 1, 2, 3. how much more the things of this life? Yea rather then they should go to Law, and that before Infidels, in any case depending between Brethren, he adviseth them rather to set up the meanest in the Church to hear and judge between them, 1 *Cor*. 6. 4.

4. When the Apostle directeth them upon the repentance of an offender, to forgive him, 2 *Cor*. 2. 4, to 10. he speaketh to the Brethren, as well as to their Elders to *forgive him*. As they were all (the Brethren as well as the Elders) offended with his sin: so it was meet they should all alike be satisfied, and being satisfied should forgive him: the Brethren in a way of brotherly love and Church-consent, as well as the Elders, by sentencing his absolution and restitution to the Church.

3. *Object*. But was not this Church of *Corinth* (who had all this power) a *metropolis*, a *mother Church* of *Achaia*, in which many Presbyteries, from many Churches in the villages were assembled to administer this censure?

Answ. No such thing appeareth from the story of the Church of *Corinth*, neither in the Acts (*Act*. 18.) nor from either of the Epistles to the *Corinthians*. True it is, *Corinth* was a *mother-city*, but not a *mother-Church* to all *Achaia*: and yet it is not unlikely that other Churches in that region, might borrow much light from their gifts; for they abounded, and were *enriched with* variety of all *gifts*, 1 Cor. 1. 5. 7. But yet that which the Apostle calleth the *Church of Corinth*, even the *whole Church* was no larger, then was wont to *meet together in one place, one congregation*, 1 Corinth. 14. 23.

A fourth and last *Argument* to prove the *Proposition*, that everie Church so furnished with officers (as hath been said) and so carried on in truth and peace, hath all Church power needfull to be exercised within themselves, is taken from the guilt of offence, which lieth upon every Church, when any offence committed by their members lieth uncensured and unremoved. Christ hath something against the *Church of Pergamus*, for *suffering Balaam* and the *Nicolaitans*, Revel. 2. 14, 15. and something against the *Church of Thyatira*, for *suffering Jezabel*. Now if these Churches had not either of them sufficient power to purge out their own offenders, why are they blamed for toleration of them? yea, why are not the neighbour Churches blamed for the sins of these Churches? But we see, neither is *Pergamus* blamed for tolerating *Jezabel*, nor *Thyatira* for tolerating *Balaam*, nor *Smyrna* for tolerating either. Indeed what Christ writeth to any one Church, his *Spirit* calleth *all the Churches* to hearken unto, and so he doth our Churches also at this day: not because he blamed them for the toleration of sins in other Churches, but because he would have them beware of the like remissenesse in tolerating the like offences amongst themselves: and also would provoke them to observe notorious offences amongst their Sister-Churches, and with brotherly love and faithfulnesse to admonish them thereof.

It is an unsound body that wanteth strength to purge out his own vicious and malignant humours. And every Church of a particular congregation, being a bodie, even a body of Christ in it self, it were not for the honour of Christ, nor of his body, if when it were in a sound and athletick constitution, it should not have power to purge it self of its own superfluous and noysome humors.

IV. Proposition. *In case a particular Church be disturbed with error or scandall, and the same maintained by a faction amongst them. Now a Synod of Churches, or of their messengers, is the first subject of that power and authoritie, whereby error is judicially convinced and condemned, the truth searched out, and determined, and the way of truth and peace declared and imposed upon the Churches.*

The truth of this Proposition may appear by *two Arguments*.

1. *Argum.* From the want of power in such a particular church to passe a binding sentence, where error or scandal is maintained by a faction; For the promise of binding and loosing which is made to

a particular church, *Matth.* 18. 18. is not given to the church, when it is leavened with error and variance. It is a received maxime, *Clavis errans non ligat*; and it is as true, *Ecclesia litigans non ligat*: And the ground of both ariseth from the estate of the Church, to which the promise of binding and loosing is made, *Matth.* 18.17,18. which, though it be a particular church (as hath been shewed) yet it is *a Church* AGREEING *together in the name of Christ*, Matth. 18. 19,20. *If there want agreement amongst them, the promise of binding and loosing is not given to them:* or if they should agree, and yet agree in an error, or in a scandall, they do not then agree in the name of Christ; For to meet in the name of Christ, implyeth, they meet not onely by his command and authority, but also that they proceed according to his Laws and Will, and that to his service and glory. If then the church, or a considerable part of it fall into error through ignorance, or into faction by variance, they cannot expect the presence of Christ with them, according to his promise to passe a binding sentence. And then as they fall under the conviction and admonition of any other sister church, in a way of brotherly love, by vertue of communion of churches; so their errors and variance, and whatsoever scandals else do accompany the same, they are justly subject to the condemnation of a Synod of Churches.

2. A second Argument to prove that a Synod is the first subject of power, to determine and judge errors and variances in particular churches, is taken from the pattern set before us in that case, *Act.* 15. 1. to 28. when certain false Teachers, having taught in the church of *Antioch*, a necessity of circumcision to salvation, and having gotten a faction to take part with them, (as appeareth by the στάσις & συζήτησις of *Paul* and *Barnabas* against them) the church did not determine the case themselves, but referred the whole matter to the *Apostles* and *Elders* at *Jerusalem*, *Act.* 15. 1, 2. Not to the *Apostles* alone, but to the *Apostles* and *Elders.* The Apostles were as the Elders and Rulers of all churches; and the Elders there were not a few, the Believers in *Jerusalem* being many thousands. Neither did the Apostles determine the matter (as hath been said) by Apostolicall authority from immediate revelation; but they assembled together with the Elders, to *consider of the matter, v.* 6. and a *multitude of Brethren* together with them (*v.* 12, 22, 23.) and after, searching out the cause by an ordinary means of *disputation, v.* 7. *Peter* cleered it by the witnesse of the Spirit to his Ministery in *Cornelius* his family; *Paul* and *Barnabas* by the like effect of their

Ministerie

Ministery among the *Gentils*: *James* confirmed the same by the testimony of the *Prophets*, wherewith the whole Synod being satisfied, they determine of a judiciall sentence, and of a way to publish it by letters and messengers; in which they *censure the false Teachers, as troublers of their Church, and subverters of their soules*; they reject the imposition of *circumcision, as a yoake which neither they nor their Fathers were able to beare*; they impose upon the Churches none but some *necessary* observations, and them by way of that authority which the Lord had given them, *verse* 28. Which pattern clearly sheweth us to whom the *Key of authority* is committed, when there groweth offence and difference in a Church. Look as in the case of the offence of a faithfull brother persisted in, the matter is at last judged and determined in a Church, which is a Congregation of the faithfull: so in the case of the offence of the Church or Congregation, the matter is at last judged in a Congregation of Churches a Church of Churches; for what is a Synod else, but a Church of Churches?

Now, from all these former *Propositions*, which tend to cleare the *first subject* of the power of the Keyes, it may bee easie to deduce certain *Corollaries* from thence, tending to cleare a parallell Question to this; to wit, *In what sense it may and ought to be admitted, that a Church of a particular congregation, is independent in the use of the power of the Keyes, and in what sense not?* For in what sense the Church of a particular congregation is the first subject of the power of the keyes, in the same sense it is independent, and in none other. Wee taking the first subject and the independent subject to be all one.

1. *Corollary.* The Church is not independent on Christ, but dependent on him for all Church-power.

The reason is plain, because he is the first subject of all Church-power, by way of soveraigne eminencie, as hath been said. And therefore the Church, and all the officers thereof, yea, and a Synod of Churches, is dependent upon him, for all Ministeriall Church-power. *Ministery is dependent upon soveraignty*; yea, the more dependent they bee upon Christ, in all the exercise of their Church-power, the more powerfull is all their power in all their administrations.

2. *Corollary.* The first subject of the ministeriall power of the keyes, though it be independent in respect of derivation of power from the power of the Sword to the performance of any spirituall

administration, yet it is subject to the power of the sword in matters which concern the civill peace.

The matters which concern the civill peace, wherein Church-subjection is chiefly attended, are of foure sorts.

1. The first sort be *civill matters*, τὰ βιωτικὰ, the *things of this life*, as is the disposing of mens goods, or lands, lives, or liberties, tributes, customes, worldly honours, and inheritances. In these the Church submitteth, and referreth it self to the civill State. Christ as minister of the circumcision, refused to take upon him the dividing of inheritances amongst brethren, as impertinent to his calling, *Luke* 12. 13, 14. *His Kingdome* (hee acknowledgeth) *is not of this world*, Joh. 18. 36. Himself payed tribute to *Cæsar*, (Mat. 17. 27.) for himself and his Disciples.

2. The second sort of things which concerne civill peace, is the *establishment of pure Religion, in doctrine, worship, and government*, according to the word of God: as also the reformation of all corruptions in any of these. On this ground the good Kings of Judah commanded *Judah to seek the Lord God of their fathers*, and to worship him, according to his own statutes and commaundments: and the contrary corruptions of strange gods, high places, Images, any Groves, they removed, and are commended of God, and obeyed by the Priests and people in so doing, 2 *Chron.* 14. 3, 4, 5. 2 *Chron.* 15. 8. to 16. 2 *Chron.* 17. 6. to 9. 2 *Chron.* 19. 3, 4. 2 *Chron.* 24. 4, 5, 6. 8., 10. 2 *Chron.* 29. 3. to 35. 2 *Chron.* 30. 1. to 12. 2 *Chron.* 34. 3. to 33. The establishment of pure Religion, and the reformation of corruptions in Religion, doe much concerne the civill peace. If Religion be corrupted, there will bee *warre in the gates*, Judg. 5. 8. and *no peace to him that commeth in, or goeth out*, 2 Chron. 15. 3, 5, 6. But where Religion rejoyceth, the civill State flourisheth, *Hagg.* 2. 15. to 19. It is true, the establishment of pure Religion, and reformation of corruptions, pertain also to the Churches and Synodicall Assemblies. But they goe about it onely with spirituall weapons, ministery of the Word, and Church-censures upon such as are under Church-power. But Magistrates addresse themselves thereto, partly by commanding and stirring up the Churches and Ministers thereof to goe about it in their spirituall way: partly also by civill punishments upon the wilfull opposers and disturbers of the same. As *Iehosophat* sent *Priests and Levites*, (and them accompanied and countenanced with *Princes* and *Nobles*) *to preach and teach in the Cities of Judah*, 2 Chron. 17. 7, 8, 9. So

Iosiah

Iosiah put to death the idolatrous Priests of the high places, 2 King. 22.20. Nor was that a peculiar duty or priviledge of the Kings of *Iudah*, but attended to also by heathen Princes, and that to prevent the wrath of God against the Realme of the *King and his sons*. Ezra 7.23. Yea, and of the times of the New Testament it is prophesied, that in some cases, capitall punishment shall proceed against *false Prophets*, and that by the procurement of their *neerest kindred*. Zach. 13.3. And the execution thereof is described, *Revel.* 16.4. to 7. where the *rivers and fountains of waters* (that is, the Priests and Jesuits, that conveigh the Religion of the Sea of Rome throughout the countreys) *are turned to blood*, that is, have *blood given them to drink* by the civill Magistrate.

Neverthelesse, though we willingly acknowledge a power in the civill Magistrate, to establish and reform Religion, according to the word of God; yet we would not be so understood, as if wee judged it to belong to the civill power, to compell all men to come and sit down at the Lords table, or to enter into the communion of the Church, before they be in some measure prepared of God for such fellowship. For this is not a *Reformation*, but a *Deformation* of the Church, and is not according to the word of God, but against it, as we shall shew (God willing) in the sequell, when we come to speak of the disposition or qualification of Church-members.

3. There is a third sort of things which concern the civill peace, wherein the Church is not to refuse subjection to the civill Magistrate, in the exercise of some publick spirituall administrations, which may advance and help forward the publick good of Civill State according to God. In time of warre, or pestilence, or any publick calamity or danger lying upon a Common-wealth, the Magistrate may lawfully proclaim a Fast, as *Iehosaphat* did, 2 Chron. 20.3. and the Churches ought not to neglect such an administration, upon such a just occasion. Neither doth it impeach the power of the Church to call a Fast, when themselves see God calling them to publick humiliation. For as *Iehosaphat* called a Fast: so the Prophet *Ioel* stirreth up the Priests to call a Fast in time of a Famine, threatning the want of holy Sacrifices, *Ioel* 1.13,14.

It may fall out also, that in undertaking a warre, or in making a league with a forraine State, there may arise such cases of conscience, as may require the consultation of a Synod. In which case, or the like, if the Magistrate call for a Synod, the Churches are to yeeld him ready subjection herein in the Lord. *Iehosaphat* though hee

H 2 was

was out of his place, when he was in *Samaria* visiting an idolatrous King: yet he was not out of his way, when in case of undertaking the war against *Syria*, he called for counsell from the mouth of the Lord, by a Councell or Synod of Priests and Prophets, 1 *Kings* 22. 5, 6, 7.

4. A fourth sort of things, wherein the Church is not to refuse subjection to the civill *Magistrate*, is in patient suffering their unjust persecutions without hostile or rebellious resistance. For though persecution of the Churches and servants of Christ, will not advance the civill peace, but overthrow it; yet for the Church to take up the Sword in her own defence, is not a lawfull means of preserving the Church-peace, but a disturbance of it rather. In this case, when *Peter* drew his Sword in defence of his Master, (the Lord *Jesus*) against an attachment served upon him, by the officers of the high Priests and Elders of the people: our Saviour bade him *put up his sword into his sheath again*; for (saith he) *all they that take the sword, shall perish by the sword*, Mat. 27. 50, 51, 52. where he speaketh of *Peter* either as a private Disciple, or a Church-officer, to whom, though the power of the keyes was committed, yet the power of the sword was not committed. And for such to take up the sword, though in the cause of Christ, it is forbidden by Christ: and such is the case of any particular Church, or of a Synod of Churches. As they have received the power of the keyes, not of the sword, so the power of the keyes they may, and ought to administer, but not of the sword. Wherein neverthelesse we speak of Churches and Synods, as such, that is, as church-members, or church-assemblies, acting in a church-way, by the power of the keyes received from Christ. But if some of the same persons bee also betrusted by the civill State, with the preservation and protection of the Lawes and Liberties, peace and safety of the same State, and shall meet together in a publicke civill Assembly (whether in Councell or Camp) they may there provide by civill power (according to the wholsome Lawes and Liberties of the countrey.) *Ne quid Ecclesia, ne quid Respublica detrimenti capiat.* If King *Saul* swear to put *Jonathan* to death, the Leaders of the people may by strong hands rescue him from his fathers unjust and illegall fury, 1 *Sam.* 14. 44, 45. But if *Saul* persecute *David*, (though as unjustly as *Jonathan*), yet if the Princes and Leaders of the people will not rescue him from the wrath of the King, *David* (a privat man) will not draw out his sword in his owne defence, so much as to touch the Lords anointed, 1 *Sam.* 24. 4. to 7.

To

and the Power thereof. 53

To conclude this *Corollary*, touching the subjection of Churches to the civill State, in matters which concerne the civill peace, this may not bee omitted, that as the Church is subject to the sword of the Magistrate, in things which concern the civill peace; so the Magistrate (if Christian) is subject to the keyes of the Church, in matters which concerne the peace of his conscience, and the Kingdome of heaven. Hence it is prophesied by *Isaiah*, that Kings and Queens, who are nursing fathers and mothers to the Church, *shall bow down to the church, with their faces to the earth*, Isai. 49. 23. that is, they shall walk in professed subjection to the ordinances of Christ in his Church. Hence also it is that *David* prophesieth of a *two-edged sword, (that is, the sword of the Spirit, the word of Christ, put into the hands of the Saints* (who are by calling the members of the Church) as to subdue the Nations by the ministery of the Word, to the obedience of the Gospel, (*Psal.* 149. 6, 7.) so *to bind their Kings with chains, and their Nobles with fetters of iron, to execute upon them the judgement written,* (that is, written in the Word) *Psal.* 149. v. 8, 9.

3. A third *Corollary* touching the independency of Churches, is this, That a Church of a particular Congregation consisting of Elders and Brethren, and walking in the truth and peace of the Gospel, as it is the first subject of all Church-power needfull to be exercised within it selfe, so it is independent upon any other (Church or Synod) for the exercise of the same.

That such a Church is the first subject of all Church-power, hath been cleared above in the opening the third Proposition of the first subject of the power of the keys. And such a Church being the first subject of Church-power, is unavoidably independent upon any other church or body for the exercise therof; for as hath been said afore, the first subject of any accident or adjunct, is independent upon any other, either for the injoying, or for the imploying (the having or the using) of the same.

4. A fourth *Corollary* touching the independency of churches, is, That a Church fallen into any offence (whether it bee the whole Church, or a strong party in it) is not independent in the exercise of Church-power, but is subject both to the admonition of any other Church, and to the *determination and judiciall*

judiciall sentence of a Synod for *direction into a way of truth and peace.*

And this also ariseth from the former discourse. For, if *clavis errans non ligat, & Ecclesia litigans non ligat*; that is, if Christ hath not given to a particular Church a promise to bind and loose in heaven, what they bind and loose on earth, unlesse they *agree together*, and *agree in his Name*, then such a Church is not independent in their proceedings, as doe faile in either. For all the independencie that can be claimed, is founded upon that promise: *What yee bind on earth, shall be bound in heaven: What yee loose on earth, shall bee loosed in heaven,* Matth. 18. 18. On that promise is founded both the independency and *security*, and *parity* also of all Churches. But if that promise be cut off from them, they are like *Sampson* when his haire was cut off, weak, and subject to fall under other men; and yet they fall softer then he did: hee fell into the hands of his enemies, but they fall under the censure of their friends. As the false Prophet recanting his error, did acknowledge, so may they: *Thus was I wounded in the house of my friends,* Zach. 13. 6. In the house of a neighbour-church or two, I was friendly smitten with a brotherly admonition, which (like *a pretious oyle*) did *not break mine head*: and in the house of a Synod of Churches, I was friendly, yea, brotherly censured and healed.

5. A fifth and last *Corollary* arising from the former discourse, touching the independencie of Churches, may be this, Though the Church of a particular Congregation, consisting of Elders and Brethren, and walking with a right foot in the truth and peace of the Gospel, bee the first subject of all Church-power needfull to be exercised within it selfe, and consequently bee independent from any other Church or Synod in the use of it; yet it is a safe, and wholsome, and holy Ordinance of Christ, for such particular Churches to joyn together in holy Covenant or communion, and consolation amongst themselves, to administer all their Church-affaires, (which are of weighty, and difficult and common concernment) not without common consultation and consent of other Churches about them. Now Church-affairs of weighty and difficult and common concernment, we account to bee

the

the *election and ordination of Elders, excommunication of an Elder,* or any *person of publick note,* and employment: the *translation of an Elder* from one Church to another, or the like. In which case we conceive it safe and wholsome, and an holy Ordinance, to proceed with common consultation and consent. Safe, for *in multitude of counsellers there is safety,* (as in civil, so in Church-affairs) *Prov.* 11.14. And though this or that Church may be of a good and strong constitution, and walk with a right foot in the truth, and peace of the Gospel: yet all Churches are not in a like athletick plight, and they will be loath to call in, or look out for help as much or more then others, though they have more need then others: yea, and the best Churches may soon degenerate, and stand in as much need of help as others, and for want of it may sink and fall into deep Apostasie, which other Churches might have prevented, had they discerned it at first.

It is also wholsome, as tending to maintain brotherly love, and soundnesse of doctrine in Churches, and to prevent many offences which may grow up in this or that particular church, when it transacketh all such things within it selfe without consent.

It is likewise an holy ordinance of Christ, as having just warrant from a like precedent. The Apostles were as much independent from one another, and stood in as little need of one anothers help, as Churches do one of another. And yet *Paul* went up to *Ierusalem* to confer with *Peter, Iames,* and *Iohn,* lest hee *should run in vain* in the course of his ministery, *Gal.* 2.2. And though in conference the chief Apostles added nothing to *Paul,* ver.6. yet when they perceived *the Gospel of the uncircumcision was committed to Paul and Barnabas, as that of the circumcision to Peter, Iames, and Iohn,* they gave unto one another *the right hand of fellowship,* ver. 9. Now then it will follow by just proportion, that if the Apostles, who are each of them independent one of another, had need to consult and confer together about the work of their ministery, to procure the freer passage to their calling, and to their doctrine: then surely Churches, and Elders of Churches, though independent one of another, had need to communicate their courses and proceedings in such cases one with another, to procure the freer passage to the same. And if the

the Apostles giving right hand of fellowship one to another, did mutually strengthen their hands in the work of the ministery: then the Elders of Churches giving right hand of fellowship to one another in their ordination, or upon any fit occasion, cannot but much encourage and strengthen the hearts and hands of one another in the Lords work.

Again, somthing might be added, if not for confirmation, yet for illustration of this point, by comparing the dimensions of the *New Jerusalem*, which is a perfect platform of a pure Church, as it shall be constituted in the Jewish Church state, at their last conversion. The dimensions of this Church as they are described by *Ezekiel* (Chap. 48. 30.) are (according to *Iunius*) *twelve furlongs*, which after the measure of the Sanctuary (which is double to the common) is about *three miles* in length, and as much in bredth. But the dimensions of the same Church of the Jewes, in *Rev.* 21. 16. is said to bee *twelve thousand furlongs*. Now how can these two dimensions of the same Church stand together, which are so farre discrepant one from another? For there be a *thousand times twelve* furlongs in *twelve thousand furlongs*. The fittest and fairest reconciliation seemeth plainly to be this, that *Ezekiel* speaketh of the dimensions of any ordinary Jewish Church of one particular congregation. But *John* speaketh of the dimensions of many particular Jewish Churches, combining together in some cases, even to the communion of a thousand Churches. Not that the Church of the Jews will be constituted in a *National* and *Diocesan* frame, with *Nationall* officers, and *Diocesan* Bishops, or the like: but that sometimes a thousand of them will bee gathered into a Synod, and all of them will have such mutuall care, and yeeld such mutuall brotherly help and communion one to another, as if they were all but one body.

If a man may say, *Theologia symbolica, or parabolica non est argumentativa*, that arguments from such parables, and mysticall resemblances in Scripture, are not valid, let him enjoy his own apprehension: and (if hee can yeeld a better interpretation of the place) let him wave this collection. Neverthelesse, if there were no argumentative power in parables, why did the Lord Jesus so much delight in that kind of teaching? And why did *Iohn*, and *Daniel*, and *Ezekiel*, deliver a great part of their prophesies in parables, if wee must take them for riddles, and not for documents nor arguments? Surely if they serve not for argument, they serve not for document.

But furthermore, touching this great work of communion and consociation of Churches, give us leave to adde this caution; To see that this consociation of Churches be not perverted, either to the oppression or diminution of the just liberty and authority of each particular Church within it self: who being well supplied with a faithfull and expert Presbyterie of their own, do walk in their integrity according to the truth and peace of the Gospel. Let Synods have their just authority in all Churches, how pure soever, in determining such Δια τάξεις, as are requisite for the edification of all Christs Churches according to God. *But in the Election and Ordination of Officers, and Censure of offenders, let it suffice the Churches consociate, to assist one another, with their counsell, and right hand of fellowship, when they see a particular Church use their liberty and power aright. But let them not put forth the power of their community, either to take such Church acts out of their hands, or to hinder them in their lawfull course, unlesse they see them (through ignorance or weaknesse) to abuse their liberty and authority in the Gospel.* All the liberties of Churches were purchased to them by the precious blood of the Lord Jesus; and therefore neither may the Churches give them away, nor many Churches take them out of the hands of one. They may indeed prevent the abuse of their liberties, and direct in the lawfull use of them, but not take them away, though themselves should be willing. The Lord Jesus having given equall power to all the Apostles, it was not lawfull for eleven of them to forbid the twelfth to do any act of his office without their intervention. Neither was it lawfull for the nine, who were of inferiour gifts, to commit the guidance and command of all their Apostolique administrations unto *Peter, James* and *John, who seemed to be Pillars.* And that, not onely because they were all (one as well as another) immediately guided by the Holy Ghost: but because they were all equall in office, and every one to give account for himself unto God.

A Caution.

I It

It is the like case (in some measure) of particular Churches; yea, there is moreover a three-fold further inconvenience, which seemeth to us, to attend the translation of the power of particular Churches in these ordinary administrations, into the hands of a Synod of Presbyters, commonly called a *Classis*.

1. The Promise of *Binding and Loosing*, in way of Discipline, which Christ gave to every particular Church (as hath been shewed) is by this means not received, nor injoyned, nor practised by themselves immediately, but by their Deputies or Over-seers.

2. The same promise which was not given to Synods in acts of that nature (as hath been shewed in the Chapter of Synods) but in acts of another kinde, is hereby received and injoyned, and practised by them, and by them only, which ought not to be.

And, which is a third inconvenience; The practice of this power of the Keys only by a Synod of Presbyters, still keepeth the Church as under nonage, as if they were not grown up to the full fruition of the just liberty of their riper yeers in the dayes of the Gospel. For a mother to bear her young daughter in her arms, and not to suffer it to go on its own feet, whilest it is in the infancie, is kindly and comely: but when the Damosell is grown up to riper yeers, for the mother still to bear her in her arms, for fear of stumbling, it were an unnecessary burthen to the mother, and a reproach to the Virgin; Such is the case here : The communitie of Churches (according to the Hebrew phrase) is as the *Mother*; each particular Church is as the *Daughter*. In the old Testament, while the Church was in her nonage, it was not unseasonable to leave the whole guidance and bearing thereof in the hands of their *Tutors and Governours, the Priests and Levites*, and in the communitie of the Nationall Courts. But now in the dayes of the New Testament, when the Churches are grown up (or should be grown at least) to more maturity, it were meet more to give the Church liberty to stand alone, and to walk upon her own legs; and yet in any such part of her way, as may be more hard to hit right upon, as in her

her Elections, and Ordinances, and Censures of eminent persons, in office; it is a safe and holy and faithfull office of the vigilancie of the communitie of Churches, to be present with them, and helpfull to them in the Lord. And at all times when a particular Church shall wander out of the way, (whether out of the way of truth, or of peace) the communitie of Churches may by no means be excused from reforming them again into their right way, according to the authority which the Lord hath given them for the publike edification of all the severall Churches within their Covenant.

Soli Christo, Τῷ Α, ἢ Τῷ Ω.

This is licensed and entred according to Order.

FINIS.

CPSIA information can be obtained at www.ICGtesting.com
Printed in the USA
LVOW02s1244180713

343500LV00001B/12/A